SOME
SEVENTEENTH-CENTURY
WORTHIES

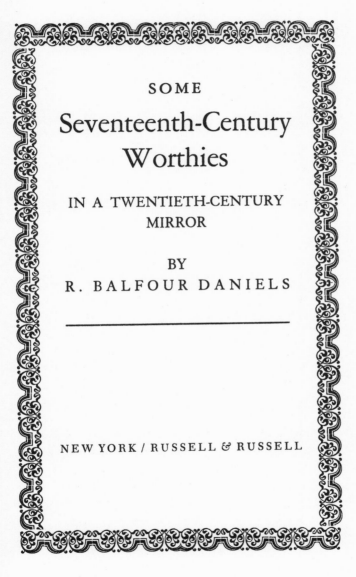

SOME

Seventeenth-Century Worthies

IN A TWENTIETH-CENTURY
MIRROR

BY
R. BALFOUR DANIELS

NEW YORK / RUSSELL & RUSSELL

TO

MY PARENTS

Acknowledgments

In PRESENTING this book to the reading public the author desires to express his obligation to Professor Alexander M. Witherspoon, who aroused his interest in these characters and read most of the essays in their original form. Acknowledgment should be made to the editors of *Voices* and *The Educational Leader* for their courtesy in allowing the republication of some of the following papers; and the helpfulness and assistance of authorities at the Sterling Memorial Library, Yale University, and at the Rice Institute Library should be acknowledged.

To Professor George M. Harper I owe an especial debt of gratitude for his kindness in reading the manuscript and giving me his invaluable criticism.

R. BALFOUR DANIELS

The University of Houston
September, 1939

CONTENTS

[ix]

SOME
SEVENTEENTH-CENTURY
WORTHIES

A Cavalier Letter Writer

LETTER WRITING is such a necessary and habitual practice in the life of almost every literate person that it is sometimes difficult to detect precisely the moment when it becomes an art. The purely business letter, we may assume, is lacking in elements necessary for it to be called literature. At the opposite pole is the entirely fictitious type of letter used merely as a device on which to hang a story. Richardson, Smollett, and Fanny Burney—to mention but three names—used a series of letters as the framework for a novel; and *Pamela, Humphrey Clinker,* and *Evelina* are indeed works of art. But no one in his right senses would consider their authors chiefly notable as letter writers on the basis of these works; for the letters are so obviously untrue to life, as letters, and so remarkable in detail and in the quality of narrative power, that they are at once dismissed as a mere device of the novelist.

Another type of letter immediately occurs to one,

the kind that is frequently found in biographies and autobiographies. One sees several imposing volumes with gilt letters on their backs, proclaiming them to be "The Life and Letters of So-and-So." These are quite likely to be interesting but often liable to be deadly. When the writer is a man in public life, they may bear a certain historical interest; if he is a writer and critic, they may have a certain literary interest; but as independent artistic creations they may be strangely disappointing.

Love letters should never be published; and it is a wise law that makes them as well as all other epistles the literary property of the writer. It is one of our few rights of privacy remaining in this age of the demon news photographers and the electric telephone. Yet the telephone is in some ways a blessing to careless letter writers; for it prevents the writing of many a foolish letter. Unfortunately the executors, next of kin, and descendants of some men and women, lacking delicacy or inspired by a sordid hope of undeserved gain, have allowed the love letters of their decedents to be published, more is the pity. Nothing can cure the writers of these letters. One can only quote the lawyer who capped the aphorism, "Do right and fear no man," with his own, "Don't write and fear no woman."

No doubt Dr. Johnson would have insisted that a good letter must contain sense. With all due respect to the learned doctor, I think we may extend the office of the letter to the realm of nonsense. Above all things a good letter should give pleasure; and if nonsensical whimsies and mad meanderings please the correspondent, let us by all means be mad and nonsensical. In the matter of all scandal and bawdry we must be governed by good taste and the laws of the realm. They were best avoided altogether; and let the writer beware also of a feeble and ineffectual euphemism whenever he is tempted to use one.

The familiar letter, if it is to be published, should not be too serious. No man would take upon himself the character of Polonius, and that is exactly what Lord Chesterfield does in writing to his son. A certain amount of jocularity is a pleasing spice to a letter. Consider a master in this vein.

Sir John Suckling, the Cavalier poet, a letter writer of true charm and distinction, reasoned with his tongue in his cheek and showed himself a merry and gallant gentleman. His letter to "a cousin who still loved young girls, and when they came to be marriageable, quitted them and fell in love with fresh" is a delight to the reader. It appears that this letter was written at the request of the father of the young cousin, who wished that his son "might be persuaded out of the humor and marry."

"Why delighted with the first knots of roses?" asks Sir John; and he reproves his cousin for not caring for them "when they come to blow." With an admirable display of wit he also warns him against widows. At the end of the letter he deals with marriage as one might expect of a Cavalier: "I should have persuaded you to marriage, but to deal ingenuously, I am a little out of arguments that way at this present. 'Tis honorable, there's no question on't; but what more, in good faith, I cannot readily tell."

A love letter to "Aglaura" is certainly not a letter of a man in love. Therefore it is printable. It is all of a piece with,

> "When, dearest, I but think on thee,
> Methinks all things that lovely be
> Are present, and my soul delighted."[1]

It contains the remarkable question: "Those tyrants, business, honor, and necessity, what have they to do with you and I [*sic*]?" and asks, "Why should we not do love's commands before theirs whose sovereignty is but usurped upon us!" Such a letter must needs be read in the same spirit in which it was written. It betokens no broken hearts but a gay and fleeting devotion.

Again Suckling writes to a friend to dissuade him from love. He advises travel; or if that be too harsh, the constant company of his beloved; or perhaps "a jolly glass and right company"; but marriage he considers too severe a remedy. He writes from Hol-

[1] Although these lines have been attributed to Suckling, they were probably written by Owen Feltham.

land and considers the inhabitants so ugly that he says, "I should spoil my prose to let in a description of them." And he likes not the situation of the country and the heavy taxes.

He is equally delightful in a letter to a friend advising him not to marry a widow whom the friend had formerly been in love with and quitted; in a mock-diplomatic epistle from the wine-drinkers to the water-drinkers; and in a burlesque sermon on malt. Everywhere one finds the same light touch, the same derisive wit coupled with a constant good humor. He is at all times the conscious artist; but nevertheless in his art he delineates his own character. Perhaps it is impossible for the users of fountain pens and typewriters to see life as Sir John Suckling saw it; but if they would write witty and readable familiar letters, let them try to recapture the Cavalier spirit in letter writing.

Some Seventeenth-Century
Books of Wonders

THE LITTLE-TRAVELED paths of literature are often
tempting. Sometimes they lead us to the mountain
ranges where some giant of letters lies sleeping; but
more often they lead nowhere in particular and end
in some charming woodland glade without a distant view in any direction. If a reader follows Matthew Arnold and devotes himself solely and with
singleness of purpose to "the best that has been
thought and said in the world," he will, presumably,
avoid these tangled bypaths and read devotedly and
with earnest contemplation only the classics, ancient
and modern. His constancy should be rewarded,
and he will prove no doubt a nobler animal. For
some of us, however, the obscure and half-forgotten
writers of a bygone age hold a dangerous fascination. The curious, the odd, and the bizarre qualities in their works may weave their hypnotic spell
about us and bewitch us as completely as Circe did
the sailors of Ulysses. The danger is that we may

become capricious and eccentric and that in following will-o'-the-wisps we may neglect the good, the true, and the beautiful.

Accordingly, let me state at the beginning that the books I propose to deal with are only moderately good, are filled with obvious and patent untruths, and are beautiful neither in form nor in expression. They contain no full-length portraits, no blushing heroines, no pictures of wild romantic scenery; but they are filled with wonders, prodigies, curiosities, and rarities aplenty.

In the year 1650 there was printed in London by Bernard Alsop, "dwelling near the upper Pump in Grub Street," an English translation of Pedro Mexia's *Silva de Varia Leccion*. It was translated by Joshua Baildon and entitled *The Wonders of the World, Discovering Many secret Rarities, that have been hidden since the Creation;* but the translator did not have the original Spanish text before him. He had a French version by Claude Graget called *Diverses Leçons*. This little book—the English edition contained only one hundred and thirty-four pages—treated a great variety of topics. There are thirty-four chapters; the titles of some of them are as follows: "Why men lived longer in former ages than now in these days," "That the sign of the Cross was in estimation before our Saviour Christ was crucified," "Of two women—the one of which in the habit of a man was made Pope, the other Em-

press," "Of men that are bred in the sea and some
other things of note," "Of divers wonderful things,"
"Of a strange medicine wherewith Faustina was
cured of dishonest love and of divers other remedies
against that passion." Other chapters deal with
speech, with sleep, with prayers, with medicinal
waters, and with many other subjects. A writer in
the *Nouvelle Biographie* describes the book thus:
*"Dans ces Diverses Leçons toutes sortes de sujets sont
passées en revue; mais aujourd'hui on peut à peine
lire quelques pages de cette compilation indigeste où
des dissertations soi-disant scientifiques et des ré-
flexions morales sont entremêlées à des traits d'his-
toire (la plupart apocryphes)."*

The credibility of this book may be judged from
the following extracts taken from Chapter XI, "Of
Men that are bred in the Sea, and some other things
of note":

"It is one marvelous thing, and that which
draws men into a deep contemplation of the
works of God, the great diversity of Fishes in
the Sea, and likewise of the Beasts of the Earth:
Pliny, Albertus Magnus, Aristotle, and divers
other Philosophers treat much of them. I know
very well, that a reasonable man is found nowhere, but upon the earth, and men inhabit
not in the water; Nevertheless I have read,
there are fishes in the sea that have the shape
of a man, amongst which there are male and
female; and the female hath the very form of

a woman, and are called *Nereides,* and the male *Tritons*. . . . *Pliny* saith, That in the time of the Emperor Tiberius, the inhabitants of Lisbon, a town in Portugal, (then famous, and is yet,) sent Ambassadors to the Emperor, to certify to him, that they had seen one of these Tritons retire and hide himself, sometimes in a cave near the sea, and that there he made music with the shell of a fish."

Possibly, in the reign of Tiberius, fishermen had not the reputation for unveracity they have since acquired, or perchance they failed to distinguish fact from fancy, when like Wordsworth, they longed to

"Have sight of Proteus rising from the sea;
    Or hear old Triton blow his wreathèd horn."

Several other authorities are cited by Mexia, among them Alexander of Alexandria and Peter Gellius, who affirm the existence of mermen and mermaids; and he concludes: "A thing therefore so approved, and by so many authors, and that all the world holds for a certain, ought not to be reputed a lie, but held for a truth."

There is one chapter on ancient marriage customs. Cicero, Pliny, and Plutarch are the authors from whom the Roman marriage customs are taken, and these need not detain us. The Babylonian practice is mentioned, by which it appears they brought their daughters on a certain day to a public place in the city. The fairest brought no dowry with them but were given in marriage to the men who would give the most money to have them. The less beautiful were treated in a similar fashion until they came to the ugliest of all, who was given with a dowry to him who would take the least; and this portion proceeded out of the money given by those who took the most beautiful at a high price. "And by this means," says the writer, "the foul ones are as well married as the fair ones, without giving any money."

Mention is also made of a town in Africa called Leptine, where it was the custom for a wife, on the day when she first entered her husband's house, to send to her mother-in-law a request that she lend her an earthen pot. This the mother-in-law would refuse to do in order that her daughter-in-law might, from the first day, learn to endure and bear with her.

The chapter ends with the following paragraph on polyandry among the Arabs:

"The Arabs of Arabia the happy, had anciently a custom, that the married wife was common to all the kindred of the husband; and as *Strabo* saith, when any of them went to her, he left at the entry of the door a little wand, that if any other should come, he might know the place was taken up, and that he must not enter: for they had that respect one to another; and he was punished with death, which entered in to a woman if he were not of kindred. Now it happened that a very fair and beautiful woman was for that cause often visited by the kindred of her husband, by means of which importunity and frequent visitation, she set at her door a little wand, to the end that whosoever should come, should think that there were another before him; and by this deceit, for many days, no man entered, till one day all the kindred and the husband were together in one place, one of them resolved to leave the rest and visit her, and finding the wand at the door, and knowing that he had left all the rest of the kindred together, thought that some adulterer had been with her; wherefore he went presently to advertise the rest, and especially the husband, who being come thither, found her all alone, and confessed the cause why she had done so; which when they considered, and found that her intention was grounded upon virtue, to the end to shun the dishonest conversation of so great a number of kindred of her husband's, and also to live in greater temperance and chastity, which was contrary to the brutish use and custom of the country, and having in their opinion just reason for what she did, she was rather praised and commended than blamed."

Among other things of which the book tells are: the esteem in which the sign of the cross was held before the crucifixion of Christ, by the Arabians and also the Egyptians, who engraved it upon the breast of images of their god Serapis; the mad love of a

young Athenian for a marble statue;[1] King Xerxes'
foolish love for a plane-tree; why man goes up-
right; how necessary water is to the life of man and
how to know that which is good; and the amity and
enmity of certain birds, beasts, and fishes. Many
curious phenomena are noted in this last-mentioned
chapter, which would deserve the scorn of the exact
naturalist. The true and the false are haphazardly
mingled together in such a manner as to justify the
epithet *dissertations soi-disant scientifiques,* hereto-
fore quoted. One is informed that "the horse is
afraid more of a camel than of any other beast";
and it is also written: "The adder if he seeth a man
cloathed, he will hurt him if he can and hath bold-
ness to venture at him; but if he see him naked, he
flieth from him." Yet the most curious statement
in the chapter concerns a tree—one reads: "The
Olive hath a natural property against the luxurious
and fleshly given, so that if an unchaste woman plant
them they die, and take no root."

The English edition of this strange book was
dedicated to Paul Holdenby, Esquire, who first gave
a copy of the French version to the English redactor;
and it was published by John Downam.

The original Spanish edition was published in
Seville in 1543. Pedro Mexia, the author, was born
in that city about 1496 and died in 1552, the year in

[1] This of course suggests the Pygmalion myth, but here the occur-
rence is reported as a fact.

which Graget's French translation of the book appeared.

II

Another collection of curiosities and natural phenomena, quite different from Mexia's *Wonders,* is *Britannia Baconica* or *Rarities of England, Scotland, and Wales* by Joshua Childrey. The complete title of this work, which was published in London in 1661, is, *Britannia Baconica: Or, The Natural* RARITIES *of England, Scotland, & Wales. According as they are to be found in every Shire. Historically related, according to the Precepts of the Lord Bacon; Methodically digested; and the Causes of many of them Philosophically attempted, with Observations upon them, and Deductions from them, whereby divers Secrets in Nature are discovered, and some things hitherto reckoned Prodigies, are fain to confess the cause whence they proceed.* It also states on the title page that it is "Useful for all ingenious men of what Profession or Quality soever."

In one respect this book resembles Thomas Fuller's *Worthies of England;* for the rarities are classified by shires, and something is told of the products and the natural features of each county. Yet these sections differ greatly as to length; while there are more than twelve pages devoted to Gloucestershire and almost as many to Kent, Radnorshire and Montgomeryshire are treated in a sentence or two. They seem to have contained fewer rarities. The author says of them: "*Radnorshire.* This shire hath sharp and cold air, because of the snow lying long unmelted under the shady hills, and hanging rocks, whereof there are many. *Montgomeryshire.* This shire bred excellent horses in times past. There is nothing else rare, or observable here for our purpose."

The book is a collection of facts and fables indiscriminately thrown together and contains as well several reflections on astrology. Although Childrey purports to have followed as nearly as he could the precepts of Lord Bacon and names his book after that distinguished writer, it is quite evident that his intelligence was far inferior to Bacon's, his credulity much greater, and his skill as a writer considerably less. Far from imitating Bacon, it is doubtful whether Childrey really understood the philosophical method of that great genius. Francis Bacon could say truly:

"I possessed a passion for research, a power of suspending judgment with patience, of meditating with pleasure, of assenting with caution, of correcting false impressions with readiness, and of arranging my thoughts with scrupulous pains. I had no hankering after novelty, no blind admiration for antiquity. Imposture in every shape I utterly detested. For all these reasons I considered that my nature and disposition had, as it were, a kind of kinship and connection with truth."[2]

[2] Translation by E. A. Abbott: *Francis Bacon* (London, 1885), p. 37.

The Reverend Joshua Childrey, on the evidence submitted in the *Rarities,* could say none of these things. Instead he has the appearance of a credulous and garrulous gossip. Whatever his virtues were, they did not consist in a passion for experiment and ascertaining the exact fact. Yet if he mentions some strongly improbable event, he is not likely to do so on his own authority although occasionally he neglects to give us the source; for example, in writing of Hampshire he says: "Our *Chroniclers* tell us, that in the year 1176 in the *Isle of Wight,* it rained a shower of blood for two hours together"; and in writing of Loch Lomond in Scotland he reports:

> "In this *Loch* (saith *Ortelius*) are thirty islands, whereof divers have villages inhabited and churches; and one of them, which is very good for the feeding of cattle, floats up and down in the lake, as it is carried by the wind: not unlike those islands reported by *Pliny* to be in the Lake *Vadimon,* which are full of grass, and covered over with rushes and reeds, and swim up and down in the Lake. There are the like also near St. *Omars* by Calais."

Pliny, it would seem, was an author whose veracity in these matters the compiler would never doubt. Indeed, all things that were related by the ancients and were not obviously myths, seem to have been readily accepted by Childrey. We find no accounts of Tritons or Nereids, it is true; but had any been reported in British waters, a description of them would have certainly been given. As an unscientific physical geography and naturalist's history of Britain, this volume is fairly interesting; but only a small portion of the work is based on the observations of the author; and often the authorities he cites cannot be credited.

The section on Shropshire is devoted chiefly to astrology, and the position of the planets is mentioned at the time of the sweating sickness in that part of the country. Yet the author disagrees with Cambden that this was thirty-three years after the first appearance of a similar epidemic in 1484; for both Godwin and Stow inform him that it was but thirty-two years later. It is a noteworthy fact that Childrey seems to manifest a desire for accuracy and exactness only in matters of astrology—of all things —wherein he considered himself somewhat skilled although he admitted that "the most important maxims in the art are many of them shrewdly to be suspected."

The mineral and vegetable products of Shropshire that he mentions I pass over; but one well-authenticated fact of which he speaks should be noted: this is the reference to old Thomas Parr of Alderbury, who lived to be one hundred and fifty-two years old and died in the year 1635. This case of longevity, which is also mentioned in a third book to be discussed in this paper, has been remarked by many writers and is said to be well attested. Nor was this happening so remote; for Old Parr had died only twenty-five years before Childrey wrote the *Britannia Baconica* or *Rarities*.

III

English readers, eager for curiosities, were to see before the close of the century a work which entirely eclipsed these earlier books on strange phenomena; it was *The Wonders of the Little World* by the Reverend Nathaniel Wanley. It had the subtitle, *A General History of Man,* and was divided into six books. The first edition, folio, appeared in 1678 and was dedicated to Sir Harbottle Grimston, a baronet who had denounced Archbishop Laud in the House of Commons and rebuked Cromwell for coercing Parliament. This book was intended to illustrate in anecdotal fashion the prodigies of human nature. Though a well-planned compilation, it shows its author to have been a man whose wide reading was only exceeded by his unbounded credulity. He was not, like Sir Thomas Browne, concerned with disproving or correcting "vulgar errors," but set down indiscriminately the strange and curious wonders about which he had heard and read. Yet Wanley's authorities are given in full; and references are made to volume, chapter, and page.

Today *The Wonders of the Little World* is chiefly

known to students of literature as one of Robert Browning's source books. There he found the story out of which he fashioned that poem for children, *The Pied Piper of Hamelin*. Wanley's account is found in Book Six, Chapter XXVI. It is as follows:

"At Hammel, a town in the Dutchy of Brunswick, in the year of Christ 1284, upon the twenty-sixth day of June, the town being grievously troubled with rats and mice, there came to them a piper, who promised upon a certain rate, to free them from them all: it was agreed; he went from street to street, and playing upon his pipe, drew after him out of the town all that kind of vermin, and then demanding his wages was denied it. Whereupon he began another tune, and there followed him one hundred and thirty boys to a hill called Koppen, situate on the North by the road, where they perished, and were never seen after. This piper was called the pied piper, because his clothes were of several colors. This story is writ, and religiously kept by them in their annals at Hammel, read in their books, and painted on their windows and churches, of which I am a witness by my own right. Their elder magistrates, for the confirmation of the truth of this, are wont to write in conjunction, in their public books, such a year of Christ, and such a year of the transmigration of the children, &c. It is also observed in the memory of it that in the street he passed out of, no piper is admitted to this day. The street is called

Burgelosestrasse; if a bride be in that street, till she is gone out of it, there is no dancing suffered."

The six divisions of this work are entitled thus: "Book I. Which treats of the Perfections, Powers, Capacities, Defects, Imperfections, and Deformities of the Body of Man"; "Book II. Which treats of the Powers and Affections of the Senses of Man"; "Book III. Containing Examples of the Virtues of Mankind"; "Book IV. Concerning the Vices of Mankind"; "Book V. Containing Historical Events" (the shortest of all the divisions); and "Book VI. Containing Miscellaneous Curiosities."

In the fifth Book, Wanley devotes a chapter (Chapter III) to the succession of the bishops and popes of Rome. He mentions the woman pope, as Mexia does; but although he gives the date of her death, he omits details that the earlier writer furnishes and simply says: "Johannes the Eighth is by most confessed to be a woman, and is usually called Pope Joan. To avoid the like disgrace, the porphyry chair was ordained: she died in child-birth in going to the Lateran, A.D. 854, having sat a few months."

In another chapter is a brief biographical sketch of the long-lived Thomas Parr; and there appears in a footnote a reference to Fuller's account of the old man in his *Worthies of England*. But Wanley tells of a Yorkshireman, Henry Jenkins, who lived to be much older than Thomas Parr and died in 1670 at the age of one hundred and sixty-nine. Jenkins, it seems, was produced as a witness at the assizes to prove a right-of-way over a man's ground. He swore to about one hundred and fifty years' memory and had a good recollection of a way over the ground in question. The judge cautioned him to take care of what he swore because there were two men, each above eighty years of age, who had testified they did not remember any such way. Jenkins replied, "Those men are boys to me." The judge then asked the aged men how old they thought Jenkins was; and they answered that although they knew him very well, they did not know his age; but that when they were boys, he was a very old man. Dr. Tancred Robinson, Fellow of the College of Physicians, discovered that Jenkins, who could neither read nor write, remembered events that had taken place in the reign of Henry VIII.

There are so many things in *The Wonders of the Little World* that it would be useless to attempt a summary of them. One may read of the great modesty of King Henry the Sixth of England, Archytas, and Martia the daughter of Varro, or learn of the shameless behavior of the Reverend Doctor Shaw and the Emperors Caligula and Commodus. Tales of strange births and stranger deaths are recounted as well as many freaks of nature and history.

Two hundred and fifty years after the appearance of *The Wonders of the Little World,* the poems of Nathaniel Wanley were published for the first time, in 1928. Five of the poems had appeared in collections of seventeenth-century verse; but it was not known definitely who the author was (although some of them had been attributed to Henry Vaughan) until 1925 when Professor L. C. Martin discovered evidence proving them to be Wanley's. These verses, nearly all on religious topics, are not such as to entitle Wanley to a prominent place even among the minor poets. His lyrical poems belong to the "metaphysical" tradition; and his use of the rhymed couplet suggests the poetry of the early eighteenth century. Yet the most that Professor Martin, his discoverer, can say for him is:

"It is not claimed that Wanley was among the greater poets of his time. To make the comparisons that most naturally suggest themselves, it is clear that his lyrical inspiration is more level than that of Henry Vaughan, generally avoiding, perhaps, the steeper descents which Vaughan could make, but also missing the sublimities and the finer perceptions or 'glimpses' recorded by the Welsh poet; and though his narrative verse approaches, it never quite attains the clangor and sweep of which Dryden's was capable. Yet it also seems clear that both for its own merits and for the interests which the historian may find in it, Nathaniel Wanley's poetry deserves more attention than it could receive while it slumbered among the Harleian manuscripts."

It does not appear that Wanley's life was a particularly eventful one. His father was a mercer, and Nathaniel was born at Leicester in 1634. After attending Trinity College, Cambridge, he received his bachelor's degree in 1653 and became a Master of Arts four years later. At the age of twenty-one he married Elizabeth Burton, daughter of the town clerk and coroner of Coventry; and to them were born five children. Wanley's first charge as a clergyman was at Beeby, Leicestershire, where he remained until 1662. Meanwhile he had published *Vox Dei, or the Great Duty of self-reflection upon a Man's own Wayes* (1658), quarto. Upon the resignation of John Bryan, D.D., nonconformist vicar of Trinity Church, Coventry, Wanley succeeded him. Besides several sermons and pamphlets he published a book entitled, *War and Peace Reconciled* (1670 and 1672), a translation from the Latin of Justus Lipsius. He died at Coventry in 1680.

That the human appetite for curiosities has not abated was shown recently by the tremendous popularity of Robert Ripley's picture-book of oddities, *Believe It or Not*. Strange as it may seem, some of the same things are here recorded that interested Mexia and Childrey and Wanley. There you will see, unless my memory plays me false, an imaginary picture of Old Parr, the ancient Shropshireman. Yet today as always, Caligula at dinner with his horse, children riding on the backs of dolphins, church towers swaying when the bells are rung—these things are the raw material of literature. Some writers have lavished their skill upon them in olden times and produced histories and poems and plays of the first rank. Follows the compiler and the raconteur, who translates them and sorts them into anecdotes; and then the skilled writer finds them, melts the fact or fable in the crucible of his imagination, and the creative process begins all over again. So these collections have their use though they lack the scientific accuracy that would make them helpful to the statistician, and show a deficiency in that form and polish necessary to make them literary classics. We should not, therefore, scorn, even though we cannot praise or greatly admire, that curious and humble writer, the compiler of prodigies.

Izaak Walton and the Ideal World

The Compleat Angler with all its fishing lore so charmingly presented, its gems of poetry, and its fair picture of simple country pleasures, depicts an ideal world that is far removed from the life of to-day and did not exist even in Izaak Walton's time. Happy and idyllic as Walton's fishing excursions may have been, it is too much to believe that the inns he encountered had at one and the same time a hostess who could cook a chub to perfection, soft beds with linen smelling of lavender, excellent ale and barley wine, and pleasant company. Nor can the critical reader give credence to the account of milkmaids and their mothers so delighted at the gift of a chub that they offered the fisherman a sillabub of new verjuice and sang songs written by Kit Marlowe and Sir Walter Raleigh.

Even Walton's showers are mild and afford an opportunity for pleasing discourse between the angler and his pupil. There is, in short, nothing to destroy the pastoral perfection of the scene. It is, to use the hackneyed phrase of the guidebook and the fishing club prospectus, "a fisherman's paradise." Alas, such pleasant places, charming scenes, and undiluted joys are found only in the imagination; and there, I think, lies the true secret of Walton's famous book. Others might tell us how to fish, how to make flies, what bait to use, where certain fish are found, what their habits are, and how to prepare them for the table; but Walton transports us to another world; he tells us not what fishing is but what it ought to be.

There is a certain amount of truth in what he says about the character of the fisherman. We may expect the angler to be a mild-mannered man and a good companion; but here, too, Walton's enthusiasm carries him into paths where we follow with our imagination rather than our reason. In writing of the angler's character, he reminds us that four of Christ's disciples were fishermen. This, to say the least, is somewhat beside the point. Fishermen, it is true, they were; but they were not anglers. Instead of following a trout stream with rod and line they took fish from a sea in nets. Furthermore, they were professional fishermen before they were professional evangelists. Yet there is a measure of truth in Walton's contention; for one associates the qualities of humanity and gentleness with a fisherman, be he professional or amateur, far more readily than with, for example, a butcher. Indeed, the associations of this last calling are liable to be unpleasant; and on this account the following announcement of a certain steamship company seems to me highly suggestive and tactless: "Dogs, cats and monkeys should be caged before being brought on board and placed in charge of the butcher, who will take care of them during the voyage at a customary fee."

Ever since Walton's time clergymen, stockbrokers, and men in various other walks of life have favored us with books on angling. None is so good as *The Compleat Angler*—and I dare say no one will ever write a book on fishing to surpass or even equal it; but they have one quality in common, these piscatorial volumes, a persistent and damnable optimism. Fishing and melancholy seem to be antagonistic. What we need is a thoroughly pessimistic treatise on fishing. Perhaps this is too much to expect. With what delight would I peruse a book entitled, *A Conservative Democrat's Day with President Roosevelt, or Disappointments on the Gulf of Mexico*. Unfortunately such a book will never be written.

Since I am not one of those who spend many golden hours seeking the trout and salmon in lake and stream, I shall not attempt to join the ranks of the writing anglers; but for the thoroughly pessimistic fisherman, if such there be, I offer a few suggestions. This writer will attack the subject from an entirely new angle, a superrealistic one. He will record in all their details the difficulties and disappointments of a day's fishing. Before he sets out on his expedition he will be put to the great inconvenience of obtaining a license. This will cause him no end of trouble; for the town clerk will be exceedingly hard to find. He will proceed to a trout stream and find long stretches of it posted and the rest fenced in with difficult strands of barbed wire. He will find casting is not easy, and his line will become entangled in the trees. A shrewish farmer's wife will object to his trespassing; and the farmer's ill-tempered dog will take a nip at his legs. His lunch will fall out of his basket and be lost in a whirlpool. The whole day's fishing will result in the catching of two small trout which will have to be thrown back because they are under the size the law allows one to take. He will be pursued by an ugly bull while crossing a pasture. The rain will descend in torrents, drenching him to the skin. On the way home one of the tires on his car will blow out; and he will be badly bitten by mosquitoes while putting on the spare. His exertions will make him tremendously thirsty, and the roadside stand near-by will supply him with lukewarm lemon pop. He will arrive home badly sunburned, only to find that his wife has eloped with a neighbor and his house has burned down.

If the writer has a mind to intersperse verses between his solemn stretches of prose, he can no doubt find many doleful dirges by consulting the melancholy Celtic bards. As for the rest, the Russian writers are perhaps the best models. But enough—I have offered many, perhaps too many, suggestions to guide the ultramodern and un-Waltonian angler. It occurs to me that possibly his world, too, does not exist.

Some Remarks on Richard Crashaw

FOR ONE BROUGHT up in the Protestant faith, an attempt to pass judgment on the poems of Richard Crashaw would be, perhaps, unwisely presumptuous. Sooner would I see a heavy-handed blacksmith come forth sooty from his stithy to repair a delicate Swiss watch. At the same time, there are probably thousands who profess the same faith and worship at the same shrine that Crashaw did, but who are even more incompetent in this than I. Yet this is not strange; for of all the devotional poets of his time Crashaw is perhaps the most difficult to understand. He demands not only a feeling for poetry but also a form of religious experience similar to his own if one would know exactly what he is writing about. To most of us the possession of both of these things is denied, though a number may have one of them. But they are, it seems to me, important in understanding *how* he wrote as well as *what* he wrote.

Some critics have charged Crashaw with a lack of taste and judgment and suggested that riper years would have developed these qualities. I find as much to object to in such criticism as Mr. T. S. Eliot does in the notion that Crashaw's poems showed a great but unfulfilled promise. Mr. Eliot has called Crashaw a mature artist and said that his death at the age of thirty-seven is not analogous to the death of Keats or of Shelley at a considerably earlier age. So it seems to me that when the poet's taste and judgment were given almost twenty years in which to ripen, it would be futile to look for a more mature and discriminating manner of writing in the subsequent years during which Crashaw might have lived. Yet it is quite possible that he has been unjustly accused of a lack of taste. His poems are, it is true, filled with the strange conceits that were common to the religious poetry of the time. Such a line, for instance, as, "Angels with their bottles come," may be displeasing to one's ear today; and there are other lines, which cannot be fairly quoted detached from their context, that to me are fraught with unpleasant suggestions. If the function of poetry is to give pleasure, how can this escape being a serious defect?

The answer is clear. It is the present-day reader that is at fault and not the writer. Wordsworth was once asked to alter certain lines in his poems because the images they were liable to evoke created an un-

wished for and unfortunate effect in the minds of
readers. But there again the problem is a different
one; for the persons who requested the changes
were his contemporaries and were ruled by the
thoughts current in his time. It reminds one of the
objection to the title of one of Matthew Arnold's
books, *Mixed Essays,* on the ground that it called
to mind an assortment of biscuits. In English—it is
easy to see how—the idea of confusion has become
associated with the word "mixed"; and thus it is
that such French phrases as *salon mixte* or *Compagnie de Navigation Mixte* sound strange to us.
Yet we must not forget that English words and
phrases are constantly undergoing slight changes in
meaning and suggestiveness. The pejorative sense
development of words is one of the bad features resulting from euphemisms and slang. It is the curse
of poets and may ruin for posterity many a fine
stanza and noble phrase. The metaphysical poet, the
poet whose verses are loaded with strange conceits,
may suffer grave injuries from these changes in language. But the critic should beware of accusing a
writer of lacking taste because he could not foresee
the effect his words would have on future generations. Whether Crashaw was lacking in judgment
or no, he was never lacking in delicacy; and delicacy
was a virtue often too little esteemed by the Caroline
poets.

Crashaw invites comparison with Donne. Their lives were very different, and so were their poems. Donne turned to the Church of England from the Church of Rome when it was greatly to his material advantage to do so; Crashaw became a Catholic even though it involved giving up his fellowship at Peterhouse and leaving Cambridge. Perhaps Donne was sincere; but his sincerity has been doubted; and certainly the *Eclogue and Epithalamion* for the infamous Lord Somerset requires some explanation. Be that as it may, it was not Richard Crashaw's custom to curry favor with the great and display in this a somewhat dubious sincerity. In fact, he had to leave Rome and the patronage of Cardinal Palotto because he could not wink at the vices of certain Italians in the Cardinal's retinue. When he had incurred the enmity of these men, it was unsafe for him to remain at Rome; and the Cardinal procured him some small employ at the Lady Chapel of Loretto. It was here that Crashaw contracted a fever in the summer and died.

The poems of John Donne are filled with syllogistic argument, with paradox, with reasoning, with gymnastics of the intellect; but Richard Crashaw's poems are those of the pure mystic. He does not seek to lay siege to the mind by argument. Rather does he show us the beauty and pathos of the life of Christ and His saints through tender and

mystical verses that appeal to the emotions; and in
so doing he achieves at times a wistful loveliness.

"I saw the curl'd drops, soft and slow
    Come hovering o'er the place's head,
Off'ring their whitest sheets of snow
    To furnish the fair infant's bed.
Forbear, said I, be not too bold;
Your fleece is white, but 'tis too cold."

There is something so gentle and so magical in those
lines that any objection to them must needs be far
wide of the mark; and even in his less successful
poems there is a wealth of religious feeling mingled
with a love of nature that makes them hard to
criticize.

The Church and the spirit of the Renaissance had
united some centuries earlier in Italy to produce
works of art to which the poems of Crashaw are
akin. The tender and reflective joy in the distant
spring landscapes of Giovanni Bellini and Giorgione
and the sweet sadness of the oval-faced madonnas of
Botticelli stir in us the same emotions that the poems
of Crashaw do. There is in his poetry a delicate and
flower-like quality found in the first shoots and tender buds of spring. Then too there is the ever present element of surprise. Whether they be odd conceits or no, they show the writer's great poetical
imagination and his charming originality. The
words are wedded in a perfect union to the senti-

ment. Out of the youthful sadness of the world the poet has created verse of deathless beauty.

"The dew no more will weep
The primrose's pale cheek to deck;
The dew no more will sleep
Nuzzled in the lily's neck:
Much rather would it tremble here,
And leave them both to be thy tear."

Almost any reader of poetry can appreciate a stanza like that. One does not need to have felt the religious ecstasy that Crashaw did to realize the magic of those lines. But there are, I suspect, countless beauties in Crashaw's poems that I cannot feel. Perhaps nine tenths of his work does not appeal to me. Yet poetry like the other arts can give only in proportion to what one brings to it; and no doubt there are many who see poetry and life as Crashaw did and can go with him further along the road.

A Once Great Reputation

OF ABRAHAM COWLEY the poet Denham wrote:

"To him no author was unknown,
   Yet what he wrote was all his own;
Horace's wit, and Virgil's state,
   He did not steal but emulate!
And when he would like them appear,
   Their garb, but not their clothes, did wear."

Yet there are probably no English poets whose rep-
utations have once been so high as Cowley's and
have suffered so great and so complete a decline.
There are so many English poets more deserving of
comparison with Horace and Virgil. And if Cowley took anything from Horace, it was his philosophy rather than his wit. He had evidently taken to
heart the Roman poet's delight in the Golden Mean
of the Peripatetic philosophers. Though one may
tolerate Horace's expression of this principle, it is,
when set forth by Cowley, prosaic, undistinguished,
vapid, and tiresome:

"May I a small house and large garden have;
And a few friends, and many books, both true,
Both wise, and both delightful too!"

Southey at his worst never wrote such disgusting
drivel; and one may doubt whether the poetess
laureate of any of our western states could equal its
inanity. Now in this same poem, *The Wish,* Cowley
has written another line which is, for English-speaking people at least, even worse than those already
quoted. He asks for, "A Mistress moderately fair."
This is carrying the principle of the Golden Mean
entirely too far. To the defects noted above it adds
the supreme fault of bad taste. In a narrative poem
it might conceivably have some reason for existing;
but here the line simply revolts the reader. So do
many other lines of Cowley's that might be suitable
in some other context but which are dismally in-
appropriate.

In the seventeenth century Cowley was considered
superior to Milton by contemporary critics; and Milton is reported to have expressed the opinion that
the three greatest English poets were Spenser,
Shakespeare, and Cowley. One hopes that this opinion was falsely attributed to him; for it is well nigh
impossible to believe that the author of *Paradise
Lost,* who must have realized Cowley's verse was far
inferior to the poetry of Spenser and Shakespeare,
would have linked the names of these three poets.
Whatever Milton thought about Cowley, it is cer-

tain that Dr. Johnson wrote of him as almost the
last of the metaphysical poets, "and undoubtedly the
best." It is dogmatizing such as this that destroys
the value of much of Johnson's criticism; for his remarks on the metaphysical school as a whole are
uncommonly sound. It is doubtful whether Cowley
was the second best or even the third best of the
metaphysical poets; and while Donne has become
interesting to a great many readers of the present
time, the poems of Cowley are now generally neglected. Nor is this due to popular caprice or the result of ignorant preference: the superiority of
Donne's poems amply accounts for it. Johnson, it
would seem, set too high an estimate on mere
rhetoric and deprecated in the metaphysical poets
that very quality which makes them interesting to
us, when he said that by pursuing their thoughts
to their last ramifications they lost the grandeur of
generality.

Even in Johnson's day the fame of Cowley was
declining. Johnson explains this as follows:

"His character of writing was indeed not his
own: he unhappily adopted that which was
predominant. He saw a certain way to present
praise, and not sufficiently inquiring by what
means the ancients have continued to delight
through all the changes of human manners,
he contented himself with a deciduous laurel,
of which the verdure in its spring was bright

and gay, but which time has been continually
stealing from his brows."

It is easy to condemn Cowley, as Johnson does, for
his careless versification, his unskillful phraseology,
his infrequent images, and his paucity of epithets.
There is almost no natural magic in Cowley's verse;
his conceits lack the humorous self-sufficiency of
Donne's; his Pindaric odes are all smoke and no fire,
irregular as to their lines but without any corre-
sponding emotional rhythm. To Cowley a poem
was an intellectual exercise rather than an emotional
experience. Nevertheless, without passion and without feeling he might have achieved some success
with subsequent generations if he had employed the
exact phrase, the careful rhyme, a balanced metre,
and a scrupulous taste. In spite of his absorption in
classic models, he had not the ancients' feeling for
correctness and restraint and remained merely a
writer in the "fashionable style." Thus he lacked
Ben Jonson's sense of form, the feeling of Donne,
and the vigor of Dryden.

Yet there are times when even the most wayward
of poets stumble into felicity, when the words and
metre and rhyme are all suited to the subject, when
their manner of writing fits their thoughts. Such is
the happy combination in Cowley's Anacreontics
and in some other translations. Here he is not too
serious, and his metaphysical style is perfectly
adapted to the ideas. His syllogistic manner is most

appropriate, and the rhymed octosyllabic lines are
suited to the sense. While the result is in no wise
great poetry, it is nevertheless charming verse. Thus
does he write of *Drinking:*

"The thirsty earth soaks up the rain,
    And drinks and gapes for drink again;
    The plants suck in the earth, and are
    With constant drinking fresh and fair;
    The sea itself (which one would think
    Should have but little need of drink)
    Drinks twice ten thousand rivers up,
    So filled that they o'erflow the cup.
    The busy Sun (and one would guess
    By's drunken fiery face no less)
    Drinks up the sea, and when he's done,
    The Moon and Stars drink up the Sun:
    They drink and dance by their own light,
    They drink and revel all the night:
    Nothing in Nature's sober found,
    But an eternal health goes round.
    Fill up the bowl, then, fill it high,
    Fill all the glasses there—for why
    Should every creature drink but I?
    Why, man of morals, tell me why?"

Perhaps "pursuing his thoughts to their last ramifications he lost the grandeur of generality" in this
instance (was it Anacreon's fault?); but whatever
he lost, he became beautifully specific and definite
as a poet should. It was hardly a serious question
he was propounding; and yet it is quite possible that
the sentiment of the poem might have pleased

another poet of the time, John Wilmot, Earl of Rochester, of whom we are told, that "he was for five years together continually drunk or so much inflamed by frequent ebriety, as in no interval to be master of himself."

Mr. Pepys' Account of an Actress

SINCE READING THE portions of Samuel Pepys' Diary
devoted to Nell Gwynn, I have glanced through
Mr. Otis Skinner's entertaining book, *Mad Folk of
the Theatre.* I find that Mr. Skinner, in the chapter
entitled "Mistress Nelly," has quoted almost every
important fact that the impressionable diarist set
down concerning Nell. By means of these quotations one may find out a great deal about the actress;
but to get a true picture of Mr. Pepys and some idea
of why he wrote down the things he did, one must
go to the Diary itself. It is quite possible that the
title of Mr. Skinner's book was inspired by Samuel
Pepys; for "mad" is a word he often applies to his
favorite comedians and sometimes, in a different
sense, to himself, especially when he is displeased
with the performance of a play.

A more sympathetic critic than Mr. Pepys cannot
be imagined; for he was devoted to the theatre and
to pretty women. He loved witty conversation, and

he was not offended if it was sometimes coarse. He had a taste for anecdotes and gossip and good wine. At least one story of his about Nell Gwynn has been disproved; but the incident was so characteristic of her that we cannot blame him for believing it or for setting it down even though he disbelieved it. Although Pepys was a discriminating critic of acting, his judgment as to the merits of plays seems at times erratic. He thought that Nell was a superb actress in comedy but in tragedy very, very bad.

The first mention of Nell Gwynn in the Diary is made on the third of April, 1665. On that day Pepys and his wife saw *Mustapha* acted at the Duke of York's playhouse. It was a bad play, and not even the acting of the famous Betterton redeemed it. But the fact that the King and the notorious Lady Castlemaine were there as well as two actresses from the King's playhouse kept Samuel from losing all interest in the entertainment. "All the pleasure of the play was," he wrote, "the King and my Lady Castlemaine were there; and pretty witty Nell, at the King's house, and the younger Marshall sat next to us; which pleased me mightily."

In December of the following year Pepys found it difficult to stay away from the theatre. He had often been troubled by his excessive love of pleasure and now and again had resolved to stay away from the playhouses. Yet on the seventh and eighth of this particular month he failed to overcome the

strong desire. On the latter date he went to the
King's playhouse. He hoped he would be unob-
served. "Here," he said, "I was in pain to be seen,
and hid myself; but, as God would have it, Sir John
Chichly come, and sat just by me." Though this
embarrassed Mr. Pepys, it was our good fortune, for
he saw "a good part of 'The English Monsieur,'
which is a mighty pretty play, very witty and pleasant. And the women do very well; but, above all,
little Nelly, that I am mightily pleased with the
play, and much with the House, more than ever I
expected, the women doing better than ever I expected, and very fine women."

It was not long after this that Samuel Pepys met
Nell Gwynn. It was toward the end of January in
1667 that he went with his wife to the King's playhouse to see *The Humorous Lieutenant*. He thought
it was a silly play but liked the "Spirit" that grew
very tall and then sank again to nothing. He also
liked the singing of Mrs. Knipp (or Knepp), a
friend of Samuel's who excited Mrs. Pepys' jealousy
more than a little. Mr. and Mrs. Pepys saw Knepp
after the play. He tells us how she "took us all in,
and brought us to Nelly, a most pretty woman, who
acted the great part of Coelia today very fine, and
did it pretty well: I kissed her, and so did my wife;
and a mighty pretty soul she is." They remained a
while and saw a rehearsal of some dancing for Suckling's *Goblins*. "And so," concludes Samuel, "away

thence, pleased with this sight also, and specially kissing of Nell."

Mr. Pepys' backstage experiences are invariably amusing. He was behind the scenes at the King's playhouse again on the fifth of October. At that time the rival playhouse, the Duke of York's, was attracting most of the playgoers. A play entitled *The Coffee House* was running there, and the theatre was so full that Pepys could not get in. "And so to the King's house; and there, going in met with Knepp, and she took us up into the tireing-rooms; and to the women's shift, where Nell was dressing herself, and was all unready, and is very pretty, prettier than I thought." He remained awhile and helped Knepp rehearse a part; but the effect of theatrical make-up when seen from the wrong side of the footlights did not please him: "But, Lord! to see how they were both painted would make a man mad, and did make me loathe them; and what base company of men comes among them, and how lewdly they talk! . . . But to see how Nell cursed, for having so few people in the pit was pretty."

There were times, no doubt, when Nell Gwynn's language was that of the gutter. Nor is this surprising; for that is where she had learned to speak. Her subsequent education as barmaid in a house of ill repute can hardly have purified or refined her language. Yet she had a quick wit and a ready answer.

Let us turn back for a moment to the spring of

1667 and discover, if we may, what London play-goers went to see at the King's playhouse when Nell Gwynn performed. Twice during the month of March and once in May, Samuel Pepys went to see *The Maiden Queen,* a new play of Dryden's, per-formed. It was presented at the King's playhouse and was "mightily commended for the regularity of it and the strain and wit." Mr. Pepys was tremen-dously enthusiastic the first time he saw it acted:

"There is a comical part done by Nell, which is Florimell, that I can never hope to see the like done again, by man or woman. The King and the Duke of York were at the play. But so great a performance of a comical part was never, I believe, in the world before as Nell do this, both as a mad girl, then most and best of all when she comes in like a young gallant; and hath the motions and carriage of a spark the most that ever I saw any man have. It makes me, I confess, admire her."

The next time he went to see *The Maiden Queen* it was with Sir William Penn, the father of the founder of Pennsylvania. Again Pepys was de-lighted. Of the play he wrote: "Which indeed the more I see the more I like, and is an excellent play, and so done by Nell, her merry part, as cannot be better done in nature, I think." Sir William Penn and Mr. Pepys watched the play from the pit; but glancing at the boxes, the diarist saw a displeasing sight: "By and by comes Mr. Lowther and his wife and mine, and into a box forsooth, neither of them being dressed, which I was almost ashamed of." It was unfortunate that Mr. Pepys' pleasure should have been marred by the thoughtless act of his wife in sitting in a box at the theatre and not dressing for the occasion. Just what he said to her when they got home we shall never know; for he did not record it; but I think we may safely assume that he had something to say on the subject.,

Evidently Mrs. Pepys and Sir William Penn shared Samuel's enthusiasm for *The Maiden Queen;* for on the twenty-fourth of May one discovers all three of them going to that play again. This time, one imagines, Mrs. Pepys was dressed in a manner which her husband deemed fitting. At this performance the acting of the lovely Becky Marshall, who had once sat next to Pepys at the Duke of York's playhouse, is commended as well as that of Nell Gwynn. The Diary says:

> "Saw 'The Maiden Queen,' which, though I have often seen, yet pleases me infinitely, it being impossible, I think, ever to have the Queen's part, which is very good and passionate, and Florimel's part, which is the most comical that was ever made for woman, ever done better than they two are by young Marshall and Nelly."

As a dancer Pepys preferred "little Miss Davis" to Nell Gwynn. She danced a jig after the end of *The*

English Princess at the Duke's playhouse; and one reads: "The truth is there is no comparison between Nell's dancing the other day at the King's house in boy's clothes and this, this being infinitely beyond the other."

It was the custom of milkmaids on the first of May to borrow silver tankards, weave garlands around them, and go dancing through the streets from door to door to obtain a small gratuity from each of their customers. So it was in London on that happy first of May in 1667 when Mr. Pepys went "to Westminster, in the way meeting milk-maids with their garlands upon their pails, dancing with a fiddler before them; and saw pretty Nelly standing at her lodgings' door in Drury Lane in her smock sleeves and bodice, looking upon one: she seemed a mighty pretty creature." Later in the day with Sir William Penn, he saw *Love in a Maze,* which was "but a sorry play." Yet can it be that the vision of the morning had affected Samuel's judgment? One may suspect it when he writes: "But here was neither Hart, Nell, nor Knipp; therefore the play was not likely to please me."

During that summer Nell Gwynn left the King's playhouse for a time. She had become the mistress of that dissolute young nobleman Lord Buckhurst, afterwards Earl of Dorset. Pepys heard on the thir-teenth of July that she had sent in her parts to the house and would act no more. This troubled him;

but his concern for her was not entirely unselfish. The next day was Sunday, and Mr. and Mrs. Pepys and Mrs. Turner hired a coach and four and drove to Epsom. They drank the waters and then went to the King's Head Inn. Let the Diary tell the rest of the story: "Here we called for drink and bespoke dinner; and hear that my Lord Buckhurst and Nelly are lodged in the next house, and Sir Charles Sedley with them: and keep a merry house. Poor girl! I pity her; but more the loss of her at the King's house."

The "merry house" did not last long, but something might be said concerning the merrymakers. Buckhurst, who led a very dissipated life, was a noted wit and poet of the time; and Sedley was the author of several plays, well known for his wit and profligacy. Lord Buckhurst and Sir Charles Sedley engaged in many escapades together. What was perhaps the most notorious of these had taken place some four years before. It is recounted both by Pepys in the Diary and by Dr. Johnson in his *Lives of the Poets*. Buckhurst and Sedley in company with Sir Thomas Ogle got drunk at the Cock Tavern in Bow Street. They appeared upon a balcony and showed themselves to the populace in most indecent postures. Then Sedley made a very profane and blasphemous speech and finally took off all his clothes. The crowd became indignant and attempted to force the door. This they could not do, and they finally forced the three inside by throwing stones, which broke the windows of the house. For his part in this outrage Sir Charles Sedley was fined five hundred pounds.

By the end of August, Nell Gwynn was back at the King's playhouse; but before her return Knepp had told Pepys the story of her leaving the theatre. Mr. and Mrs. Pepys and Knepp were all together on this occasion, and Mrs. Pepys was very jealous. The entry for the first of August tells us about it:

> "After the play, we [went] into the house, and spoke with Knepp, who went abroad with us by coach to the Neat Houses in the way to Chelsea; and there in a box in a tree, we sat and sang, and talked and eat; my wife out of humor, as she always is when this woman is by. So, after it was dark, we home. Set Knepp down at home, who told us the story how Nell is gone from the King's house, and is kept by my Lord Buckhurst."

Unfortunately, when Nell did return, she attempted tragedy; and her acting of tragic parts could not please even so warm an admirer as Samuel Pepys. She appeared in *The Indian Emperor;* and the diarist "was most infinitely displeased with her being put to act the Emperor's daughter; which is a great and serious part, which she do most basely." A few days later he hears "that Nell is already left by my Lord Buckhurst, and that he makes sport of her and swears she hath had all she could get of him; and Hart, her great admirer, now hates her; and that she is very poor, and hath lost my Lady Castlemaine, who was her great friend also: but she is come to the House, but is neglected by them all." Again in November (the eleventh) the Pepys family went to see *The Indian Emperor,* which is described as "a good play, but not so good as people cry it up"; and Sam adds, "I think, though above all things Nell's ill speaking of a great part made me mad." When he sees *The Surprizall* the next month he is displeased by the actors, "and especially Nell's acting of a serious part, which she spoils."

She did not like tragedy; and in the Epilogue to *The Duke of Lerma* spoke these lines:

"I know you, in your hearts
Hate serious plays,—as I hate serious parts."

And in the Epilogue to *Tyrannical Love* she said:

"I die
Out of my calling in a tragedy."

In the former play, Pepys tells us, "Knepp and Nell spoke the prologue most excellently, especially Knepp, who spoke beyond any creature I ever heard."

It was hard for Samuel to understand how this actress could excel in comedy and yet be so very poor in a tragic part. On December 28, 1667 he went with his wife to see *The Mad Couple.* He called it an ordinary play but did like the acting:

"But only Nell's and Hart's mad parts are most excellently done, but especially hers: which makes it a miracle to me how ill she do any serious part, as, the other day, just like a fool or changeling; and in a mad part, do beyond all imitation almost."

There are not many more entries in the Diary having to do with Nell Gwynn. On one occasion when he called for Knepp he saw "Beck Marshall come dressed off the stage . . . and also Nell in her boy's clothes, mighty pretty. But, Lord! their confidence! and how many men do hover about them as soon as they come off the stage, and how confident they are in their talk!"

It was not until early in 1668 that the Clerk of the Acts in the Admiralty Office heard that the King had taken any particular notice of Nell Gwynn. Then Knepp told him "that the King did send several times for Nelly and she was with him, but what he did she knows not." Several caustic words follow concerning the frivolity of Charles II and its bad effect on the state. The Diary does not tell us how Nell became King Charles' mistress and bore him two children, the titles they were given, and many other facts well known to history. Lord Buckhurst may have cast her off, but the King did not. Even on his deathbed he urged that she should be provided for.

Unfortunately the Diary had to be abandoned towards the middle of 1669 on account of Pepys' failing eyesight. The last mention he makes of Nell is on January seventh of that year. He and his wife went to the King's playhouse to see *The Island Princess*. He liked the play and wrote: "We sat in an upper box, and the jade Nell come and sat in the next box; a bold merry slut, who lay laughing there upon people; and with a comrade of hers of the Duke's house, that come in to see the play."

Never again will England see such days as those when the Merry Monarch ruled. Yet if the plagues and fires have disappeared and the Dutch fleet no longer menaces the Thames, there are gone too those joyous days when the milkmaids danced with flowery garlands on the first of May and the 'prentices rioted in the streets, when the horses' hoofs struck sparks from the cobble stones and Mr. Samuel Pepys with a friend or two sang in his garden under a rising moon.

Avaunt, Base Melancholy!

IT WAS A JUNE morning in Paris. The sun was shining, and the sky was blue, not that serene azure I had left behind me in Provence but an uncertain, capricious blue that betokened majestic white clouds and after them perhaps dark storm clouds and rain. I lay in bed reading; and as I finished a cup of chocolate, I came upon these words of Sir Thomas Browne's:

"For my conversation, it is like the Sun's with all men; and with a friendly aspect to good and bad. Methinks there is no man bad, and the worst, best; that is, while they are kept within the circle of those qualities, wherein they are good: there is no man's mind of such discordant and jarring a temper to which a tuneable disposition may not strike a harmony."

Brave words, those! And truly spoken like a philosopher, which this physician found the time and the detachment and the inclination to be. In spite of professional duties and civil strife this learned doctor remained the contemplative man and graceful writer, whose prose has lost nothing of its charm after two hundred and ninety-seven years.

But my thoughts were interrupted; for a steady hissing sound from outside made me throw down the *Religio Medici* and leap from my bed. There beneath my window I saw in the Seine a small tugboat that had stopped at the Quai des Grands Augustins. I glanced across to the island and saw the restaurant of the *Galant Vert* half hidden by the trees and the gray walls of the Palais de Justice with the spire of Sainte Chapelle peeping above. For the moment this little hissing tugboat was all mine, mine by right of discovery; and a sudden joy possessed my heart as I saw it lying there with its brass rails gleaming in the sunshine. Then as I relinquished my momentary ownership, I said: "Sail on, O little boat, bending back your tall funnel to pass beneath the Pont Saint Michel. Sail on up the Seine with your train of barges, past the solemn towers of Notre Dame to I know not what happy landing place; and be glad you are not conducting barges across the smoky, sad, and almost treeless harbor of New York."

This was such a scene as Robert Burton would have prescribed for the melancholy man; for did he not hold that "some are especially affected with such objects as be near, to see passengers go by in some great roadway or boats in a river"? And again he remarked concerning the same matter:

"A good prospect alone will ease melancholy, as Gomesius contends, *l. 2, c. 7, de Sale.* The citizens of Barcelona, saith he, otherwise penned in, melancholy, and stirring little abroad are much delighted with that pleasant prospect their city hath into the sea, which like that of old Athens besides Aegina, Salamina, and many pleasant islands had all the variety of delicious objects. So are those *Neapolitanes* and inhabitants of Genoa to see the ships, boats, and passengers go by, out of their windows, their whole cities being sited on the side of an hill, like Pera by Constantinople, so that each house almost hath a free prospect to the sea, as some part of London to the Thames."

Is it a wonder that Burton delighted to stand on Folly Bridge and listen to the bargees' profanity?

This learned man, a member of the clergy, took as great an interest in medicine as Sir Thomas Browne did in religion. Yet the amazing thing about the *Anatomy of Melancholy* is its excursions into all fields of human knowledge; for Burton seems to have been familiar with all the known philosophers, physicians, historians, poets, geographers, explorers, and astronomers who had lived and written in Europe before his time. The man was a veritable walking encyclopedia. When one thinks of the thousands of volumes he read and the countless notes he must have taken, the thought is enough to humble and subdue the aspiring scholar of today —the age of narrow specialists.

In "Air Rectified" alone the number of authorities cited and the astronomical, geographical, and philosophical lore displayed quite overwhelm the reader of the present time. Burton is advocating a change of air as a cure for melancholy, but he ranges as far as the distant planets and yet comes down again to earth and even to England. Now, in our day, one sees a different tendency. Take, for example, a writer whose interests are admittedly diverse, a modern satirist who travels with the complete *Encyclopaedia Britannica* in his trunk and whose interests include history, philosophy, music, the fine arts, and biology—Aldous Huxley, whose paramount interest seems to be human nature. He presents a notable contrast to Robert Burton although he might have resembled him had they lived in the same century. Yet it was Huxley's fate to be born in the last decade of the nineteenth century, a grandson of the famous scientist, Thomas Henry Huxley.

One might take the opening chapter of Mr. Aldous Huxley's novel *Antic Hay* and call it "Air Confined." Here there is no soaring aloft into the empyrean nor any prospect of fair cities by the banks of rivers. Instead one discovers a young man named Gumbril, master in a public school, sitting on a hard chapel bench and thinking how uncomfortable it is. What wouldn't he give for a large, inflated pneu! That starts a different train of thought, and Gumbril wonders whether one wouldn't be very comfortable with pneumatic trousers. The invention is completed and called "Gumbril's Patent Smallclothes," rather inelegant in appearance, it is true, but wonderfully adapted to cushionless seats.

When not moved by such comic fancies Mr. Huxley satirizes vulgarity by being extremely vulgar and exposes the mean and the ignoble as cruelly as Swift. Yet for all the pitiless cynicism with which he depicts hideously self-centered and small-souled characters, there has crept into his writing an element of hope. His *Eyeless in Gaza* presents a sombre enough picture of decadent society, but with a difference; for he suggests that people banded together to practice forbearance and nonresistance may yet bring peace and salvation to a war-weary world.

To return to Burton's strange book, it is a literary curiosity the like of which we shall never see again; for who is willing to spend his life in a library poring over the writings of the ancients on every conceivable subject? We seek rather the latest authority and have a feeling that a theory is likely to be right because it is new. So many ideas of the writers of old have been discredited that we look with distrust upon them all. Modern science has exploded the earlier respect for authority; but its material progress has been so great, especially in the fields of physics and chemistry, that we run to the other extreme: we embrace every new system and theory with implicit faith when its proponent comes forth from the laboratory and announces his discovery; that is, the laymen do. The discoverer's fellow scientists are more guarded in their acceptance. But they are more open-minded than their predecessors in the seventeenth century who were unwilling to recognize Harvey's discovery of the circulation of the blood because it was contrary to what was taught by Galen.

Our research has become experimental, and we seek the causes of and cures for melancholy in the psychopathic ward rather than the Bodleian Library. Perhaps this tends toward a more accurate scientific knowledge of the subject; perhaps it lays too much emphasis on the abnormal—as critics of Professor Freud contend; but however that may be, we suspect it contributes little to the advancement of literature.

Holy Dying and the Agnostic

IT IS EASY TO understand why *The Rule and Exercise of Holy Dying* by Jeremy Taylor has lost its former popularity. None of the beauties of its style, nor its scholarly manner, nor even the tender and helpful Christian sentiments expressed therein can bring this book back into favor. The reasons for this are not hard to find. In the first place, there are too many who call themselves Christians but no longer believe in the existence of a hell; and if hell does not exist, why should one be concerned with the manner in which one dies? This failure to believe in hell, as well as the disappearance of a personal devil, has had many unfortunate effects on the literature of our time. Sermons, which used to be filled with fire and brimstone, have become milder, less picturesque, and less interesting. So, too, while temptations undoubtedly still exist, it is very difficult if not impossible at present to write a dialogue between oneself and Satan, as John Bunyan did, and expect anyone to read it. Satan has become an intellectual abstraction in whom fewer and fewer people believe. Satan no longer exists as a personality, and with him all the minor devils and demons have vanished. This may or may not be a great relief to the human mind; but, in any event, literature has been deprived of another device with which to adorn its plain and obvious stories. To believe in a heaven and think that a hell does not exist, or to believe in God and not in the devil is possibly an example of wishful thinking; but be that as it may, the prevalence of heterodoxy has caused a diminishing interest in the practice of holy dying and in all writings about it.

Another reason for the present lack of interest in Jeremy Taylor is the growth of agnosticism. There are undoubtedly a great many people in our English-speaking world today who practice a sort of passive agnosticism. Many of them go to church from force of habit, because it is the accepted course of conduct in the communities in which they live, and for many other reasons. Yet at heart they are agnostics: to them holy dying means little or nothing. Perhaps the development of science in the nineteenth century has something to do with this. These people say with Huxley: "I have no faith, very little hope, and as much charity as I can afford." They believe in doing practical good as a means of ameliorating the lot of their less fortunate brothers upon this earth; but they are not in the least concerned with their own dying, holy or unholy. For them heaven is as doubtful a place as hell. They do not look for any consciousness without living nervous matter. For these persons the contemplation of death, if they happen to think very much about it, is indeed awful; and they follow the sensible plan of not thinking too much about their own death.

Yet another reason may be advanced—and it is closely related to the last—for our present neglect of the seventeenth-century religious writers; and that is, the attitude of the physicians and psychologists of today. The religion of Sir Thomas Browne could hardly be the religion of a doctor of medicine at the present time. A forgotten idiom and an obsolete philosophy cloak thoughts of his, which, though intelligible to us, seem quaint, unreal, and fantastic. Jeremy Taylor is also unacceptable to the apostle of twentieth-century science. A too-serious contemplation of death by someone who is not obviously destined to die in the immediate future is now noted by psychiatrists as a dangerous symptom incompatible with the rules of mental hygiene. The doctors, then, will do everything in their power to end such morbid fancies. Long consideration of one's approaching dissolution becomes the sign of an unbalanced mind. The patient is presently deprived of all sharp instruments, and a careful watch is kept over his actions.

To conclude, may we consider what the difference in attitude toward the things of the spirit is? To me it seems, though doubtless many members of the clergy would vehemently deny it, that we have turned from a consideration of the soul's health to the health of the mind. Perhaps someone will suggest that these two things are not mutually exclusive and are even two different phases of one and the same thing. He may be right; but nevertheless he must admit that now the emphasis is placed on the mental rather than the spiritual. We may have suffered an unfortunate loss as a result of this; but we have, I think, achieved a certain gain: we have released and scattered a great force of misdirected emotion. We are still squandering our resources, but in a different fashion.

Footnote on Biographies

THE FUTURE HISTORIAN should have no difficulty in finding materials for a lively account of our times and the prominent people who lived therein. Verily, his problem will be one of selection rather than of searching for obscure facts in the lives of forgotten men. Today we are overwhelmed by the vast numbers of biographies, memoirs, and lives pouring from the printing presses. Recent historians of early Tudors and late Windsors jostle each other on the booksellers' shelves. Newly written accounts of François Rabelais and Anatole France bewilder and confuse us; the latest book on George Washington demands the attention of a reader who has hardly had time to forget *The Strange Death of President Harding*. Yet people continue to read Boswell and Froude, Franklin and Henry Adams, not to mention Benvenuto Cellini.

This last name makes me wonder whether truthfulness is to be desired in an autobiographer. A great deal of Mark Twain's charm is due to the preposterous lies with which he filled his reminiscences. Lord Herbert of Cherbury, on the other hand, informs us in his autobiography that *he* always told the truth. Perhaps this statement was due to a faulty memory rather than any desire to appear unduly virtuous; for he tells us unblushingly of certain discreditable doings of his; but chiefly, I think, his claim to this unparalleled veracity comes from a certain naïveté common to seventeenth-century writers. In the following century this quality disappears; and we find such a writer as Franklin open and aware of his imperfections, but sophisticated. In the nineteenth century this sophistication turns to hypocrisy; but now, at last, we are back where we started: tell everything, and if it has an emetic effect, so much the worse for the reader.

In biography the writer must be guided by his artistic conscience, if he has one. Truth then becomes more important; but even so it is not necessary to rake up ancient scandals. Perhaps Izaak Walton's *Life of John Donne* touches too lightly upon the great Dean's dissolute youth; but I think the hints he gives are sufficient; for the latter part of Donne's life was really the most important. The pious serenity of George Herbert's existence was more to this biographer's taste; and there he has painted a picture with which one can find little fault.

Anthony à Wood's biographical sketches are less satisfactory. True, they are informative, fearless, interesting. Yet they lack sympathy and life. The *Athenae Oxonienses* gives us a great many facts but little insight into the lives of such men as Raleigh and Burton. They were both curious men; and their lives abounded in material for the instruction, amusement, and edification of the reader. Wood, however, has made but scant use of all the biographical matter that must have been available. He relates the bare facts and leaves almost everything to our imagination.

In an entirely different strain are the biographical ramblings of John Aubrey. His disorganized paragraphs on the lives of many famous men may omit important events and be filled with erroneous dates, but contain gossip and anecdotes aplenty. Artistically these *Lives* are inexcusable: they have no beginning or ending; they are not arranged in orderly fashion; they give no complete picture. Yet they are highly diverting on account of the anecdotes collected from various sources. When he writes about persons whom he actually knew, such as Ralph Kettel and William Harvey, he gives us a real insight into their characters; and indeed these brief essays might be called character sketches instead of lives.

To return to Lord Herbert of Cherbury, we have only to glance at his *History of the Life and Reign of King Henry VIII* to discover that he was an historian of taste and discernment. He may have painted rather too favorable a portrait of that tyrannical king; but his accounts of the military campaigns and politics of the time are exceedingly well done. His treatment of the leading political figures of the time is worthy of note. Take, for example, his account of Sir Thomas More's resignation of the Great Seal:

"Sir Thomas More, Lord Chancellor of England, after divers suits to be discharged of his place—which he had held two years and a half—did at length by the king's good leave resign it. The example whereof being rare, will give me occasion to speak more particularly of him. Sir Thomas More, a person of sharp wit, and endued besides with excellent parts of learning (as his works may testify) was yet (out of I know not what natural facetiousness) given so much to jesting, that it detracted no little from the importance of his place, which, though generally noted and disliked, I do not think was enough to make him give it over in that merriment we shall find anon, or retire to a private life. Neither can I believe him so much addicted to his private opinions as to detest all other governments but his own Utopia, so that it is probable some vehement desire to follow his book, or secret offense taken against some person or matter—among which the king's new intended marriage or the like, might be accounted—occasioned this strange counsel;

though, yet, I find no reason pretended for it but infirmity and want of health."

Sir Thomas More, according to the historian, told his family nothing of resigning the office, but appeared at his lady's pew in church the next day, hat in hand, and said, "Madam, my lord is gone," as one of the servants might formerly have done. He then explained that he had given up the Great Seal; but the jest was not appreciated by his wife and daughters. Evidently a case of "The Judicial humorist—I've got *him* on the list!"

Biography had not come into its own in England of the seventeenth century. Yet the germ of great biography was there. Writers had begun to turn their backs upon Plutarch, great biographer though he was. Aubrey, Evelyn, and Pepys were unconsciously preparing the way for a writer who was to achieve the greatest triumph possible for a biographer. When dialogue was added to anecdote and a private journal was made the means of recording the life of a great man, then that amazing life was written that placed among the immortals the name of James Boswell.

"A Pleasant Air but a Barren Soil"

So DIFFERENT in many of their ideas about education, John Milton and John Locke both protested
against one dismal feature of the school curriculum
of their time; that is, the writing of Latin themes,
orations, and verses. Locke also thought that too
much time was spent upon Latin grammar, and
that the ideal way to learn the language was to
get a tutor who could talk Latin to his pupil. Although it would have been easier to obtain such a
tutor in Locke's day than at present, the schoolboy
of that time learned Latin well but painfully. There
seemed to be a traditional feeling in that age that
the proper study of the classics must be conducted
with great severity and that a whipping now and
then was necessary to effect a proper mastery of
grammar. "Why, else," says Locke in his *Thoughts
Concerning Education,* "does the learning of Latin
and Greek need the Rod, when French and Italian
need it not? Children learn to dance and fence
without whipping; nay Arithmetic, Drawing, etc."

Yet Milton at St. Paul's and Locke at Westminster learned Latin and Greek in the traditional way. The long and difficult compositions they were compelled to write in these learned tongues irked them both. Milton, who was some twenty-four years older than Locke and wrote on the subject first, expressed his distaste thus:

"First, we do amiss to spend seven or eight years merely in scraping together so much miserable Latin and Greek as might be learned otherwise easily and delightfully in one year. And that which casts our proficiency therein so much behind is our time lost in too oft idle vacancies given both to schools and universities; partly in a preposterous exaction, forcing the empty wits of children to compose themes, verses and orations, which are the acts of ripest judgment, and the final work of a head filled by long reading and observing with elegant maxims and copious invention."

Likewise Locke said concerning a boy's education, "Yet by all means obtain if you can that he be not employed in making *Latin Themes* and *Declamations,* and least of all, *Verses* of any kind."

Herein is apparent an advantage of the physician over the poet; while the latter can protest only against the compulsory writing of *Latin* verses, the former may object to a schoolboy's writing verses of any kind. Be that as it may, the reader is not left in doubt as to Locke's reason for this objection. It was not that these *Juvenalia,* even when written in the pupil's native tongue, might possibly be devoid of merit or perchance appear to be the crude expressions of an immature mind. Rather should the youth be kept from the writing of verses because it was a bad habit and led to no good end but had disastrous consequences. Locke's own words on the subject are not to be neglected:

"For if he have no *Genius* to *Poetry,* 'tis the most unreasonable thing in the world to torment a child and waste his time about that which can never succeed; and if he have a poetic vein 'tis to me the strangest thing in the world that the father should desire or suffer it to be cherished or improved. Methinks the parents should labor to have it stifled and suppressed as much as may be; and I know not what reason a father can have to wish his son a poet, who does not desire to have him bid defiance to all other callings and business; which is not yet the worst of the case; for, if he prove a successful rhymer, and once gets the reputation of a wit, I desire it to be considered what company and places he is likely to spend his time in, nay, and estate too; for it is very seldom seen that any one discovers mines of gold or silver in Parnassus. 'Tis a pleasant air, but a barren soil."

Elsewhere he remarks that poetry and gaming usually go together and sounds a warning against both. Yet Locke can hardly have been thinking of

Milton when he said this; it would be difficult to imagine the "Lady of Christ's" rattling the dice or boisterously making an extravagant wager. Yet in all justice to Locke one must admit that Milton possibly belonged to the minority. George Herbert and Francis Quarles and William Drummond of Hawthornden led quiet, sober, and righteous lives; and there were others. But not so many years before Ben Jonson had held his "merry meetings" at the Mermaid Tavern, where a roistering crew had consumed countless gallons of Canary sack. Almost a hundred years had passed since the shocking death of Kit Marlowe, a horrible example of the effect of the writing of poetry and the consequent keeping of bad company and visiting disreputable places. Nor were Jack Donne and Tom Carew the model young men that an ideal education should produce. Was it not the writing of verses that started them on their wild careers? Rare Ben himself would have been the first to admit that mines of gold or silver were seldom discovered in Parnassus; for did he not tell Drummond that he had been "beggar'd" by the writing of poetry? At the same time Jonson would not have given up his profession of dramatist and poet and his position as literary dictator of London for anything in the world. Years before he had tried working at a trade and did not like it; no more would he have cared to be a doctor, lawyer, or merchant.

There was, strange as it may seem, one poet Locke might have quoted to enforce his point. Yet had he done so with an apt quotation, he would at the same time have weakened his case; for the affairs of that particular poet prospered, and he amassed a fortune. Nevertheless, Will Shakespeare remarked, as any rational man might:

> "The lunatic, the lover, and the poet
> Are of imagination all compact."

This indeed was no idle coupling of characters. Perhaps the truly imaginative man has at some times the qualities of each; he has his moments of lunacy when he may be the lover or the poet; he has his sane moments when he may be a philosopher like John Locke; but his imaginary devils, his imaginary beauty, his imaginary "forms of things unknown" are more real to him than all the realities of the philosophers. If he is a Shakespeare or a Newton or a Francis Bacon, his realities may in time become those of the multitude. But your true poet, though he might agree with Locke about the mines of Parnassus and though he might use the same words, would, I am sure, arrange them differently and say, "'Tis a barren soil, but a pleasant air!"

Ballads of Cavalier and Puritan

THE PERIOD OF THE Great Rebellion in England
(1640-1660) saw not a few ballad writers. Many of
their ballads have survived, and today they are interesting mainly for their political and historical significance. Their literary value is slight; and where
it *is* manifest, the subject is quite likely to be one
unconnected with politics. Love and the convivial
celebration of the charms of wine—topics that be-
guile able poets in any age—furnished material for
the best of these ballads. Some there were in honor
of King Charles, and these were often better than
the average; but at times they degenerated into un-
mitigated doggerel.

The most vehement of these ballads were scur-
rilous, libelous, obscene, and badly written. Some
were merely absurd and amusing though devoid of
literary merit.

A number of ballads were written at the time of
the Scottish rebellion of 1640. Martin Parker, whose

devotion to the King was so strong that he referred to him as "Charles the Great," wrote several of these. One is entitled *Britain's Honor. In the two valiant Welshmen who fought against fifteen thousand Scots.* It is not surprising to learn that one of the Welshmen was killed and the other captured; but one's heart cannot fail to be cheered at the thought of their valor when one reads the stirring lines:

> "Bring on their souls; these two hot shots
> Withstood full fifteen thousand *Scots.*"

Contemporary history outside of England is touched upon by the ballad writer who was moved to write of the Turkish Sultan's challenge to the Emperor of Germany and the King of Poland in the year 1640. He called his composition *The Great Turk's Terrible Challenge* and ended his stanzas with the refrain,

> "But God deliver Christians all,
> That they by such do never fall."

Beggars all a-Row by Humphrey Crouch, which was sung to the tune of *Cuckolds all a-row,* preaches the doctrine of *carpe diem* and advises one to continue to drink while a penny remains in his pocket. It seems to have no particular political significance. Another ballad written by the same author in 1642 bewails the state of the town during the civil strife. It is entitled *A Godly Exhortation* and commences thus:

"When pride aboundeth in the city
  And people's hearts are void of pity;
When little children learn to swear
  And wickedness abounds each where,
Then let God's people cry and call,
Good Lord have mercy on us all."

An anonymous ballad satirizing James I and Charles I appeared in 1645. It is libelous in the extreme, ridicules and attacks King James's family and personal habits, and advances the suggestion that Charles is not to be trusted. Rather more amusing and less abusive is John Looke's *Keep Thy Head on Thy Shoulders and I Will Keep Mine* (1641). This refers to the flight from England of Sir John Suckling, Sir Will. Davenant, Henry Percy, and Henry Jermyn. The writer voices his intention of remaining in England, and has the courage to add this rollicking chorus:

"Then merrily and cheerily
  Let's drink off our wine;
Keep thy head on thy shoulders,
  I will keep mine."

It was a sad day for England when the Puritans decided that the time-honored celebration of Christmas smacked too much of paganism and ought to be abolished. Gone then were the joyous feasting and merrymaking, the ceremonies of Yule log and banquet hall; and England was ordered to observe the anniversary of the birth of Christ in a solemn and

decorous manner. Men were advised to go about
their daily tasks as on any other day. This Puritan
Christmas was lamented by one who wrote *The
World Is Turned Upside Down* in that gloomy winter of 1646. Part of his song went:

> "You never heard the like before,
>   Holy days are despised,
>   New fashions are devised;
> Old Christmas is kickt out of town;
> *Yet let's be content, and the times lament;*
> You see the world turn'd upside down."

All manner of men were ridiculed in these spirited
ballads, and the Anabaptists came in for their share.
A young man named Samuel Oates had been going
about the country baptizing people by total immer-
sion, particularly young women, both married and
single. On some of them the exposure and cold had
disastrous effects, and one died as a result of the
baptism. Oates was tried for manslaughter, and
while he was awaiting trial a ballad was published
entitled, *The Anabaptists out of order or The Relation of Samuel Oates, who lately seduced divers
people in the County of Essex, where he re-baptized
thirty-nine and drowned the fortieth, for which offense he now lies imprisoned at Colchester, till his
trial.* It begins,

> "From London City lately went
>   A brother of your Sect
> To Essex with a full intent
>   To visit the Elect."

In spite of this song, which accused the young man of many unspeakable deeds, he was acquitted.

Many of these pieces bewailed the economic ills of the time not without obscene similes and lewd metaphors. Among the verses of this type is, *The Good Fellow's Complaint: who being much grieved strong liquor should rise in paying a pot for excise.*

Again, others are patriotic and charming in the devotion which they show to sovereign or party or to the City of London. Among these may be listed: *O, Brave Oliver, Twelve Brave Bells of Bow,* and *A Harmony of Healths.* The last mentioned was written in 1647 and is thoroughly Royalist in its sentiments. In fact, not only the King but various members of the royal family are bravely praised. It has a delightful swing and a happy Cavalier tone to it, as the following quotation clearly shows:

> "For the best wine let's call,
>   that we can get here;
> Let's in a merry vein
>   all cares abandon,
> King Charles will come again
>   shortly to London.
> Here's to our Royal King
>   in Spanish Fountains,
> And to the blest offspring,
>   Prince of the Mountains.
> I neither dread rebukes,
>   Nor adversaries,
> Here's a Health to both the Dukes,
>   And the two Marys."

Yet, as I remarked earlier, perhaps the best of these ballads are those that do not deal with politics at all but with love. For example, *A Kiss of a Seaman* with its bewitching refrain, "For a kiss of a Seaman's worth two of another," seems to me far more sensible than Ibsen's strange play, *The Lady from the Sea,* which invests the same idea with a lot of mystical tomfoolery. Of course there is no particular reason why a nineteenth-century dramatist should handle a theme in the manner of a seventeenth-century ballad writer; but the point is this: that although the ballad may be an inferior form of art, the ballad maker has, in so far as he is able, shown a taste and decorum in his composition, which the dramatist, working with a superior literary form, has failed to exhibit. The result is a good ballad but a mediocre play; but, nevertheless, almost any man in his senses would prefer to witness the play and let the singing of the ballad go hang.

But I digress. Another love poem deserves mention. It is the *True Lover's Summons,* and it really deserves to be dignified by the name of poetry. It is so far above the average ballad found in such a collection that one forgets the companion pieces and begins immediately to think of Suckling and Lovelace. Indeed it might almost have been written by either of these excellent poets. Unfortunately the author is not known. Though the entire poem merits quotation, I give only the first stanza:

> "Sweet heart be not coy,
>   for in faith I love thee;
> Thou art my only joy,
>   now I come to prove thee.
> Though my absence long
>   may procure suspicion,
> Yet I will not wrong
>   thee in no condition,
> For I am only he
>   that loves none but thee
> Wherefore let not me
>   be of hope frustrated
> But grant love to me
>   for which I have long waited."

With this lovely lyric in mind, it may be as well to take our leave of Cavalier and Puritan ballad writers, though there are many other phases of their art that could not fail to interest us, not to mention the circulation and influence of these songs and the fascinating woodcuts with which they were illustrated.

George Herbert's Literary Executor

A SHORT TIME BEFORE George Herbert's death, his friend, Nicholas Ferrar, hearing of Herbert's illness, sent Mr. Edmund Duncon from Little Gidding to see Mr. Herbert and inquire after his health and to assure him that daily prayers were being offered at Gidding for his recovery. Mr. Duncon found the invalid quite weak but deeply interested in the health and welfare of his friend Ferrar. When these questions had been answered, Herbert said: "Sir, I see by your habit that you are a priest, and I desire you to pray with me." They joined in prayer, and then Mr. Duncon departed promising to return in five days.

On his return Mr. Duncon found the sick man much weaker and feared that death was not far off. Herbert asked the messenger to give Nicholas Ferrar an account of him and to request that the prayers at Gidding in his behalf be continued. Then he handed Mr. Duncon the manuscript of a volume of

poems entitled *The Temple* and said: "Sir, I pray
deliver this little book to my dear brother Ferrar,
and tell him he shall find in it a picture of the many
spiritual conflicts that have passed betwixt God and
my Soul, before I could subject mine to the will of
Jesus my Master, in whose service I have now found
perfect freedom; desire him to read it; and then, if
he can think it may turn to the advantage of any
dejected poor Soul, let it be made public; if not,
let him burn it: for I and it are less than the least
of God's mercies."

After the death of his friend, Nicholas Ferrar
decided to publish *The Temple* and sent the manuscript to Cambridge, where the Vice Chancellor re-
fused to license it unless the lines,

>   "Religion stands a Tip-toe in our Land,
>   Ready to pass to the American strand"

were eliminated. Ferrar, however, was unwilling
to have his friend's book published unless it were
allowed to stand exactly as written. There were
some arguments on both sides, and finally the Vice
Chancellor allowed it to be licensed.

Strangely enough it does not appear that George
Herbert and Nicholas Ferrar saw one another during the three years of the former's ministry when
most of the poems in *The Temple* were doubtless
composed. Izaak Walton has described their rela-
tions as follows: "Mr Ferrar's and Mr Herbert's

devout lives were both so noted that the general report of their sanctity gave them occasion to renew that slight acquaintance which was begun at their being Contemporaries in Cambridge; and this new holy friendship was long maintained without any interview, but only by loving and endearing Letters."

Nicholas Ferrar was born in London on the twenty-second of February, 1593. He was an extremely studious and pious child; and, according to Walton, he is said to have been called Saint Nicholas at the age of six years. Before the end of his thirteenth year he entered Cambridge, being a pensioner at Clare Hall. In 1606 this was not an unusually early age at which to enter the university, and Ferrar doubtless found a number of other students there no older than himself. In 1608 George Herbert came up to Trinity; but beyond the "slight acquaintance" that Walton mentions there is no record of any friendship between Ferrar and Herbert at this time. Nicholas Ferrar acquired the reputation of being a very studious youth; and it was said that in the winter his window was the first to show a light in the morning and the last to display one at night. He was awarded the degree of Bachelor of Arts in 1610 and soon thereafter was elected a Fellow of Clare Hall.

Unfortunately his health at this time was not of the best: he was subject to frequently recurring attacks of ague. These attacks became so severe in 1613 that he was advised to leave England immediately and attempt to regain his health by means of foreign travel. Although his M.A. degree would ordinarily have not been awarded until the summer of that year, an exception was made in his case, and he was granted the degree three months before the usual time.

A place was procured for him in the household of the Princess Elizabeth, who had just become the bride of the Elector Palatine. To Nicholas Ferrar a courtier's life was not particularly attractive, and when the princess left Holland, he resigned his place in her household. From the Hague and Amsterdam he proceeded to Hamburg, where he was overwhelmed by the hospitality of the English merchants there. They were charmed by his conversation but probably somewhat amused by his attempt to elevate the tone of their discourses and his avoidance of all spirituous liquors. At Leipsic, which he next visited, he remained several months engaged in studious pursuits. Here, it is interesting to note, he found it useful to learn a system of artificial memory.

The next summer Ferrar set out again on his travels. He visited Prague and several other cities before he reached Vienna. The plague was prevalent in southern Germany, and he did not tarry long in any of these places but set out for Venice in the middle of the winter of 1615. He spent Easter in Venice and then took up his residence at Padua, where he devoted himself chiefly to the study of medicine. During his stay in Italy he made a secret visit to Rome. Fear of the Inquisition led him to change his lodging every night; but one day when he mingled with a throng in the Vatican to see the Pope pass by, he neglected to kneel with the rest of the crowd. Fortunately for him he was forced to his knees by one of the Swiss guards, who cried, "Down, rascal, down!" Shortly after this he returned to Venice and from there went to Marseilles.

At Marseilles he was again attacked by the fever and almost died. He wrote to his friend Garton in Venice, asking him to come to Marseilles immediately. Garton hastened to the bedside of his friend and found him on the road to recovery. He remained until Ferrar had regained his health.

Not long after this Nicholas Ferrar set sail for Spain. The monotony of the voyage was broken by an encounter with a pirate ship. The pirates had a much larger vessel and were rapidly overtaking the little ship on which Ferrar was a passenger, when a council was called to decide whether they should surrender or join battle with the pirate craft. Ferrar's opinion was asked, and he bravely replied, "Let us fall into the hand of God, and not into the hands of men." They were preparing to fire on the pirate ship, when it turned about and sailed away in pursuit of a much larger vessel which had just come into view.

Upon landing Nicholas proceeded immediately to Madrid and arrived there somewhat earlier than he had expected. On account of his early arrival there were no letters or money awaiting him; but he did discover through an acquaintance of his family that there was certain trouble at home that necessitated his presence. Accordingly he gave up his plan of a visit to France and at once set out for England. His money had not arrived, and he was unwilling to accept a friend's offer of a loan. So he sold his cloak and some jewels and started on foot for San Sebastián, two hundred miles away. This journey was not without dangerous adventures, and he finally reached the coast without any money whatsoever. He accepted a loan of £10 from an English factor and set sail for Dover. When he reached home after an absence of five years, it is said that his father did not recognize him at first. Yet he and the rest of the family were overjoyed at the return of Nicholas.

At this time Nicholas Ferrar's father was a shareholder in the Virginia Company, which had been founded twelve years before. He was also interested in the New Bermuda Company, an allied organization. John Ferrar, Nicholas' brother, was a member of the Council of Virginia. Thus it was that during the next seven years of his life Nicholas Ferrar was principally engaged in the affairs of these companies. The Virginia Company prospered; and its success was in no small measure due to the able management of Sir Edwin Sandys, who unfortunately incurred the displeasure of the King. The King, in spite of the patent that had been granted, attempted to force Sir Edwin out; and the majority of the shareholders resisted this attempt. Finally, under the influence of the Lord Treasurer Cranfield and the Spanish party at the court, the King permitted an investigation to be made of the conduct of the company's affairs.

Nicholas Ferrar was now deputy treasurer of the Virginia Company, and with Lord Cavendish and Sir Edwin Sandys defended the company against the accusations of its enemies. Nevertheless suit was brought against them, and it was finally decided "that the patent or charter of the Company of English merchants trading to Virginia, and pretending to exercise a power and authority over his Majesty's good subjects there, should be thenceforth null and void." Over a hundred members of the defunct Virginia Company were in the House of Commons, including Sandys and Ferrar. Although they could not revive the company, they were resolved to impeach the Lord Treasurer who had been instrumental in its destruction. Ferrar, who later bitterly regretted it, played a leading part in the impeachment, the result of which was that the Lord Treas-

urer, Earl of Middlesex, was found guilty, imprisoned, fined, and rendered incapable of again sitting
in the House.

Even though the Virginia Company had been dissolved, Nicholas Ferrar might have become, had he
desired to, a great figure in the world of affairs. He
was a member of the party in power, a friend of
its influential leaders, in short, a young man with
a promising future in politics. He had, however,
mapped out for himself and his family a life of
retirement and religious devotion. He had put aside
all thoughts of marriage and taken vows of celibacy;
and now that he had taken holy orders he resolved
to seek no preferment in the church and not to
aspire to anything higher than the deaconate. His
mother, now a widow seventy years of age, purchased an estate known as Little Gidding, twelve
miles from Huntingdon. Here it was that she settled with her son Nicholas, her son John and his
wife and child, and her son-in-law Mr. Collett and
his family. The Collett family was quite large;
there were eight sons and eight daughters. A daughter was born to the John Ferrars after their removal
to Gidding, and she was named Virginia.

It is remarkable that these good people after their
life in London could submit to a program as severe
as that which Nicholas Ferrar mapped out for them;
and it is no wonder that this group of people
through their piety and devotion attracted a great

deal of attention in the England of their day. Izaak Walton and several other writers have given accounts of the daily program at Little Gidding; and indeed it was unusual.

At five o'clock all arose and said their prayers in their respective rooms. Then they dressed and went to the great hall where Nicholas waited for them. Here the younger boys and girls recited hymns and verses of the Bible which they had been given to learn. At six o'clock they all met again and said the first office of the day. This took about a quarter of an hour and consisted of a hymn, Psalms, etc. One of these offices was appointed for each hour; but since the entire household could not be present at each of these, various members were made responsible for the service at a particular hour.

They assembled in the great hall and proceeded to church three times each day, the services taking place at seven, ten, and four o'clock. The schoolmasters, of which there were three, and their pupils breakfasted after the morning service and then went to the schoolhouse; but the rest of the household had nothing to eat until eleven when they dined on the simplest food. Silence was observed during the meal, while some member of the family read aloud from an instructive book. The afternoon was broken only by frequent summonses to prayer. Supper was at six, and immediately before the meal a hymn was sung; while during the meal a chapter of the Bible was read, followed by a selection from the *Book of Martyrs*.

After supper they enjoyed a walk or some other innocent amusement until eight o'clock prayers in the great hall. After prayers the children and grandchildren of Mrs. Ferrar kneeled and asked her blessing. George Herbert, who took a great interest in the religious manner of life at Little Gidding, suggested that a constant night watch be added to the day offices. Nicholas Ferrar thought well of this suggestion, and accordingly a watch was kept every night from nine o'clock in the evening to one o'clock in the morning. Yet this was not compulsory but conducted only by volunteers; and no one except Nicholas kept the watch more than one night a week. On the nights when Nicholas rested he would have the watchers knock at his door at one o'clock, and then he would spend the remaining hours of the night in prayer and meditation. Although Nicholas Ferrar died in 1637, this manner of life was continued at Little Gidding until 1646 when Parliamentary soldiers invaded the place.

Before George Herbert became one of the clergy, he was given by Bishop Williams a prebend with which went the patronage of Leighton Ecclesia, a parish quite near Gidding. Herbert urged his friend Nicholas Ferrar to take this living; but Ferrar declined it and held to his resolve to remain a deacon. Herbert, it seems, contemplated exchanging his parish at Bemerton for one nearer Gidding; but death claimed him before this could be accomplished.

Ferrar sent Herbert his translation of the works of Juan de Valdés; and when this was published, it was with Herbert's marginal notes. So the friendship continued until the year 1633 when the lingering disease that had for so many years threatened George Herbert's life finally resulted in his untimely death.[1]

[1] Bibliographical Note: For further material in regard to George Herbert and Nicholas Ferrar one should consult *The Life of Mr George Herbert* by Izaak Walton and the anonymous *Nicholas Ferrar. His Household and His Friends*, edited by T. T. Carter.

Thomas Traherne,
A Late-Discovered Poet

IN AN AGE WHEN disillusioned young men fresh from
the universities are flooding publishers' offices with
hastily written novels and copious impressionistic
and unpolished manuscripts of verse, it is a pleasure
to come across the poems of a writer whose verses
were first published almost two hundred and thirty
years after his death. Thomas Traherne, a seventeenth-century mystic, left his poems in manuscript
when he died in 1674. It was not until the early
part of this present century—1903 to be exact—that
his poems were given to the printing press.

It is no wonder that the discoverer of Traherne's
poems took a justifiable pride in conclusively proving their authorship and giving them to the public.
I am not referring to those persons who rescued the
manuscripts from oblivion, although they deserve
their due share of praise, but to Mr. Bertram Dobell,
who first recognized Traherne as the poet and estab-
lished his authorship. Yet it seems to me that their

discoverer claims too much for these poems and that his elation over his truly remarkable literary discovery has blinded him somewhat to the defects of the poems. Traherne's discoverer would doubtless admit that Wordsworth, who also hymns the child's relation to immortal life and his intuitive knowledge thereof, is an immeasurably greater poet; but to the unbiased observer it seems that Herbert, Vaughan, and Blake are also finer poets.

Thomas Traherne is about as different from Chaucer as a poet could be. Wordsworth and Chaucer were so unlike that Matthew Arnold cautiously avoided any comparison; but Traherne has even less in common with Chaucer than Wordsworth has. Traherne's poetry is intensely subjective; it is concerned with his mind and soul, his happy childhood, and his God. Wordsworth may write about innocent children of the countryside, but with this seventeenth-century poet it is always Traherne himself who is—or was—the child. This introspective sentimentality is a serious defect. There are some persons who object to sentimentality of any kind. Yet where it is coupled with humor and a detailed and objective relation to happily conceived characters, as in Dickens' novels, it is excusable; or where it is joined with a waggish drollery, as it is throughout Sterne's writings, it is permissible. But when a poet looks within his own heart and never ceases to lament the passing of his happy and innocent childhood days, the reader is liable to become impatient and justly demand a more heroic theme.

If Traherne had been a great poet, he would have had less cause to regret his lost childhood; or, to put it in a different way, if he had retained the enthusiasm, the spontaneity, the ever-wondering and delighted eye of the child, he might have achieved great poetry. Little as we know about Traherne's life, it seems fairly certain that he was not a worldly man. In fact his *Centuries of Meditations* would seem to indicate clearly that he cared little for the things of this world. In the "Third Century," Section 46, he writes:

> "When I came into the country, and being seated among silent trees, and meads and hills, had all my time in mine own hands, I resolved to spend it all, whatever it cost me, in the search of happiness, and to satiate that burning thirst which nature had enkindled in me from my youth. In which I was so resolute, that I chose rather to live upon ten pounds a year, and to go in leather clothes, and feed upon bread and water, so that I might have all my time clearly to myself, than to keep many thousands per annum in an estate of life where my time would be devoured in care and labor."

No worldling could have made a resolve like that. Nevertheless, such a resolution was no aid to poetry. Shakespeare at the Globe Theatre, Milton busied with his Latin Secretaryship, and Donne as Dean of

Saint Paul's, for all their worldly aspirations, found a fuller life and a life better suited to the writing of great works. It is true that Milton's chief poems were written late in life when he no longer was involved in affairs of state and that Donne's best work was completed early; but neither of these men sought to withdraw from life and seek a solitary happiness. Even George Herbert, whose pious impulses more nearly coincide with those of Traherne, had seen something of the world and at the last was busily engaged in the affairs of his parish.

It is unfortunate that we do not know more of Traherne's life in London as chaplain to Sir Orlando Bridgeman, but it is hard to believe that this mystical poet took any great delight or relish in the life of the capital. But worldly or not, had he retained the enthusiasm of youth and the childlike, imaginative eye and impulse, as the others did, he might have become a great poet.

It is clear that there was at the base of Traherne's philosophy a certain unalterable selfishness which was bound to hamper rather than aid him in life as in literature. It is definitely expressed in the words, "That I might have all my time clearly to myself." Had he, like Robert Burton, spent all this time in the Bodleian Library, he might have given us another book like the *Anatomy of Melancholy;* but Thomas Traherne could never have done that. He loved too dearly the country and the mountains to spend his whole life pouring over dusty tomes.

Although he achieved some success in charming irregular metres, Traherne's mastery of the technique of verse was faulty. His catalogues of objects are interesting and foreshadow Whitman's use of the same device, and his fancy sometimes delights us; but his verse is somewhat labored and requires too many auxiliary words. Take for example the following lines from the poem *News:* "So much it did my heart inflame," and "Or else did bear them on their wings," and "And crown of all which round about did lie."

Seldom if ever does Traherne achieve the high magic that one finds in Vaughan, and he never displays the melodious perfection of the Cavalier poets. At the same time one cannot find in his poems the sweet reasonableness and calm piety of George Herbert. Instead Traherne voices a wistful Celtic yearning, imperfectly expressed, it is true, but nevertheless plaintive and mystical. He is the restless and disappointed spirit looking back at the idealized joys of childhood and looking forward with longing to the perfect peace that lies beyond the grave. Such a poet is a poet of moods, or possibly of one mood; and if the reader cannot sympathize with him in that, he cannot appreciate him at all; for Traherne's audience must always be a small one; and where the craftsmanship of the great artist is lacking, there must be something that transcends his art and touches our emotions to make us admire and cherish and rescue from oblivion the poems of a sadly strange and unvenerated poet.

The Wisdom of Sir Thomas Browne

ALTHOUGH SIR THOMAS BROWNE was much given to aphorisms, proverbs, old saws, and wise sayings, he cared little for worldly wisdom or mundane rules for the conduct of life. To him death was a more interesting subject than life, and the spirit of man seemed as important to him as man's body. One is not surprised therefore to find him considering the conduct of one's affairs from a deeply religious vantage point. "Honesty is the best policy" is an expression of a sentiment almost as foreign to the writings of Sir Thomas Browne as it is to the Sermon on the Mount. On the contrary this idealistic physician says: "Be not beneficent for a name or cymbal of applause; nor exact and punctual in commerce for the advantages of trust and credit, which attend the reputation of just and true dealing: for such rewards, though unsought for, plain virtue will bring with her, whom all men honor, though they pursue not."

The sentence just quoted reminds one of Matthew 6:2, where Christ is reported to have said: "Therefore when thou doest *thine* alms, do not sound a trumpet before thee, as the hypocrites do in the synagogues and in the streets, that they may have glory of men. Verily I say unto you, They have their reward."

Though he gives much good advice in *A Letter to a Friend,* at no time does Sir Thomas Browne base his counsel on material grounds. Instead he scorns the man who is virtuous merely to avoid practical difficulties. Christ's extension of the Seventh Commandment to include libidinous thoughts and desires is echoed in the *Letter* thus: "He that is chaste and continent not to impair his strength or terrified by contagion will hardly be heroically virtuous."

From the Sermon on the Mount we have: "Give to him that asketh thee, and from him that would borrow of thee turn not thou away"; while the *Letter* admonishes: "Be charitable before wealth makes thee covetous, and lose not the glory of the mitre." "Lose not the glory of the mitre" seems equivalent to "lay up for yourselves treasures in heaven."

Follows then Sir Thomas Browne's surprising discovery that, "A slave unto Mammon makes no servant unto God," a sentence in which any improvement over the translators' "Ye cannot serve God and Mammon," is not apparent. Coming to the praise of sincerity and wholehearted devotion to the good, the learned physician says: "Persons lightly dipt, not grained, in generous honesty are but pale in goodness and faint-hued in sincerity. But be thou what thou virtuously art, and let not the ocean wash away thy tincture." How much more forceful is the following: "For I say unto you, That except your righteousness shall exceed *the righteousness* of the scribes and Pharisees, ye shall in no case enter into the kingdom of heaven."

If it were not already evident that Sir Thomas Browne had the Sermon on the Mount in mind when he wrote the *Letter,* the reader would realize this was the case when he read: "Be not a mere Gamaliel in the faith, but let the Sermon on the Mount be thy Targum unto the law of Sinai."

Sir Thomas Browne evidently believed that what was worth saying was worth saying a number of times and that what had been said concisely might much better be said sonorously. So if a distinctive phrase pleased him once, he did not hesitate to use it again even though this might make him appear to be quoting himself. Thus in his *Urn Burial* he says: "But the long habit of living indisposeth us for dying"; and in the *Letter* he declares: "The long habit of living makes mere man more hardly to part with life, and all to be nothing, but what is to come." Thus he states the obvious in terms so stately and majestic that the unwary reader may easily suspect he has just encountered some profound truth. The hypnotic effect of Sir Thomas Browne's prose is quite disarming, and unless the reader is on his guard he will not detect the worthy doctor's lapses into ridiculous and superstitious nonsense. On the other hand, the religious beliefs set forth in his writings represent no mere lip service to a creed of which Sir Thomas Browne was entirely sceptical. They are the profound and passionate beliefs of an idealist and a Christian, who in spite of his discouraging and disheartening experiences had an implicit faith in the perfectability of man.

II

To find fault with the writing of Sir Thomas Browne, on whose style so many able English authors have modelled their own, would, in an age used to harsh-sounding and unmusical prose, seem churlish indeed. It is not my purpose to discuss his style, nor do I intend to show wherein its perfection lies. Of greater interest to me is the state of mind and the habit of life which limited and even hindered Sir Thomas Browne in his dealing with certain problems.

The physician's knowledge of the body made him despise it; and instead of praising and encouraging all forms of physical activity, he became deeply interested in questions of man's spirit and devoted much time to the study of philosophy. "There is," he says, "I think no man that apprehends his own miseries less than myself, and no man that so nearly apprehends another's. I could lose an arm without a tear, and with few groans, methinks, be quartered into pieces."[1] Yet he is always concerned about the fate of his soul, a strange state of mind for a medical man. He is deeply troubled in the matter of his own salvation, for he tells us:

> "The number of those who pretend unto salvation, and those infinite swarms who think to pass through the eye of this Needle, have much amazed me. That name and compellation of *little Flock*, doth not comfort but deject my devotion, especially when I reflect upon mine own unworthiness, wherein, according to my humble apprehensions, I am below them all."[2]

He shows as much concern over things spiritual as Robert Burton does over matters physiological. That he was a believer in spirits and devils, then, is not surprising; and as for the credence that he gave astrology, it was no more than the belief of most men of his time. The golden sunlight of the learning of the ancient world was softened and also somewhat dimmed by the misty cloud of medievalism. In their excessive respect for the older authorities and the ancient books, many scholars forgot to look at the life about them. Some physicians, it is true, notably William Harvey, were exploring the

[1] *Religio Medici*, part II, section 5.
[2] *Ibid.*, part I, section 56.

human body and making important discoveries; while Sir Thomas Browne, oblivious to much that was going on around him, speculated strangely on the sepulchral urns lately found in Norfolk and the custom of urn burial in general.

If he shows in his works a despite of the body and a glorification of the spirit, he also displays little concern for the study of human beings. He seems to take more interest in the habits and customs of the ancient Britons, Greeks, Romans, and Hebrews than in the lives of the people about him. He manifests a quaint bookishness and a pedantry exceeded only by his contemporary Robert Burton. He is not concerned with the hopes and fears, the loves and hates and follies of the man of his day. For womankind he cares even less. "I never yet cast a true affection on a Woman,"[3] he says; and it is not difficult for the reader to believe him and consider his advice sincere when he says:

> "I was never yet once, and commend their resolutions who never marry twice, not that I disallow of second marriage; as neither in all cases of Polygamy, which considering some times and the unequal number of both sexes may be also necessary. The whole world was made for man, but the twelfth part of man for woman: man is the whole world and the breath of God, woman is the rib and crooked piece of man."[4]

[3] *Ibid.*, part II, section 5.   [4] *Ibid.*, section 9.

After marriage his views may have changed considerably; and one is compelled to wonder whether he is quite truthful when he writes, "I speak not in prejudice, nor am I averse from that sweet sex, but I am naturally amorous of all that is beautiful." Is he exaggerating when he says he could "look a whole day with delight upon a handsome picture, though it be but of an Horse"? Coupled with his remarks about the fair sex, as it is, this last statement might be taken to be a piece of fine irony; yet so serious is the tone and so earnest is the argument of this book, that I for one am uncertain as to the author's intent.

Certainly Sir Thomas Browne appears to be quite sincere in the wish that mankind could multiply like the trees without any union of the sexes. Sir Kenelm Digby takes him to task for this ungallant desire and remarks:

"*Plato* taxed his fellow *philosopher,* (though otherwise a learned and brave man) for not sacrificing to the *Graces;* those gentle female goddesses. What thinketh your Lordship of our Physician's bitter curse of that action which *Mahomet* maketh the essence of his *Paradise?* Indeed besides those his unkindnesses, or rather frowardnesses, at that tenderhearted Sex (which must needs take it ill at his hands) methinketh he setteth marriage at too low a rate, which is assuredly the highest and divinest link of human society. And where he

speaketh of *Cupid* and of *Beauty,* it is in such a
phrase as putteth me in mind of the Learned
Greek Reader in *Cambridge* his courting of his
Mistress out of *Stephens* his *Thesaurus*."

It is the ever-besetting temptation of the scholar
to withdraw too much from the world of men and
women and to inhabit another world far removed
from ordinary life. The writer, if he desires to give
any human quality at all to his writings, should at
least be an observer of the life about him if not an
actor in the drama of life. It was this temptation
that Sir Thomas Browne was unable to resist; and
as he lost touch with reality, he became more interested in a future and problematical existence.
Here was one who deliberately turned his back on
the English Renaissance and looked behind it into
the Gothic shadows of the Middle Ages.

Such a man, naturally enough, reaches the heights
when he is writing not of life but of death. The
pleasing aphorism and the graceful phrase recur
most often when he is considering departure from
this earthly life; while with Bacon, as one might
expect, it is the mundane and practical affairs of life
that are dealt with in a pithy and aphoristic manner.
But our physician Browne is a veritable Janus, looking to the past and to the future, living in the time
but not of it, saying that "the long habit of living indisposeth us for dying" and wondering what man's
long sleep will be like. In his *Urn Burial* one finds

these words: "Were the happiness of the next world as closely apprehended as the felicities of this, it was a martyrdom to live; and unto such as consider none hereafter, it must be more than death to die, which makes us amazed at those audacities that durst be nothing and return to their chaos again."

His love of a retired life is even influenced by what he sees beyond the grave; and well might he rejoice that he had no part in the civil strife about him; for he says: "Happy are they whom privacy makes innocent, who deal so with men in this world that they are not afraid to meet them in the next; who, when they die, make no commotion among the dead, and are not touched with that poetical taunt of Isaiah."

Two more short quotations will suffice: "There is no antidote against the opium of time, which temporally considereth all things: our fathers find their graves in our short memories, and sadly tell us how we may be buried in our survivors." And of time and death he says: "The number of the dead long exceedeth all that shall live. The night of time far surpasseth the day, and who knows when was the equinox? Every hour adds to that current arithmetic, which scarce stands one moment."

But Sir Thomas Browne, in spite of the sad beauty of his prose, has touched but lightly the eternal tragedy of the life and death of man. He has neglected altogether its dramatic aspect. One objects that he was not writing plays and could not be expected to treat the subject as Shakespeare did in *Macbeth* or to consider life as the author of *Samson Agonistes* considered it. That indeed was not necessary; for in a wider sense Plato and the writers of the gospels have depicted this tragedy as well as, if not better than, all others. They have done it through the medium of simple spoken language. There is, then, a greater and more moving manner of writing than the majestic, cypress-garden prose of Sir Thomas Browne. It is the simple and sincere word falling from man in the Valley of the Shadow of Death. He who recaptures it has written for all time; and until this world crumbles into nothingness and books are no more, will men read the last words of Socrates and of Christ.

Francis Quarles' EMBLEMS as Seen in the Twentieth Century

PIETY IN THESE latter days has almost ceased to exist; and now the apparently pious soul, unless he be an elderly person known beyond question to be sincerely devout, is often as not suspected of hypocrisy. It is an age of romantic longings and cynical despair, in which our greatest heroes and adventurers, our conquerors of the air and of the polar regions, achieve their ends mainly through the use of machinery and a thorough knowledge of the machine. War has become mechanized and regrets the passing of the cavalry charge of old; a sail upon the horizon is to the sailor merely a reminder of an age gone by. Is it a wonder, then, that people have ceased worrying about the state of their souls? They look to Science to preserve them from evil in body and mind; Religion they make a clearinghouse for philanthropic projects; their conduct rests upon a basis purely utilitarian. Who in such a world—and such is the English-speaking world today—would read the *Emblems* of Francis Quarles? Who wants "a picture with a posie," a sententious bit of verse, quotations from the saints? Nobody; that is, no general reader; for one must always except the religious devotee, the pale scholar, and the antiquary. The class to whom Francis Quarles once made a great appeal could not read him today, although they delight in inspirational versifiers far inferior to Quarles, whose place among religious poets is far from high. In many cases, it would seem, literacy is a doubtful blessing.

The most arresting thing about Quarles' *Emblems* from viewpoint of the present time is, to be sure, the pictures. I think few people would deny that they are faintly absurd, probably the last thing in the world they were intended to be. Surely they are quaint and often most entertaining. Fascinating little cherubs appear engaged in various occupations reminding one of the lovely little Cupids that once adorned the walls in Pompeii. In the backgrounds of the pictures one sees various strange things: a skeleton with bow and arrow, a house on fire, a head in the clouds blowing on the water with puffed-out cheeks, or as the poet says in a rather labored alliterative line, "And blustering Boreas blows the boiling tide." How feeble this is compared with Shakespeare's, "Blow, winds, and crack your cheeks!"

To me the most interesting illustration is the tenth

of Book I. There Cupid and Mammon (the latter
being dressed in the fashion of a gentleman of the
period) are playing at bowls. Their backs are to the
onlooker; and in the middle distance stands Satan
directing the game; while at the farther end of the
bowling green waits Dame Fortune with a fool's
cap, which is to be the victor's crown, in her hand.
The reader is not left in doubt as to the meaning of
the allegory; for in the accompanying poem Quarles
explains that the bowls are sinful thoughts. In the
present depraved age it is difficult to take that kind
of precept seriously. It calls to mind the experience
of a campus evangelist some years ago who accosted
a student totally unknown to him with the question,
"Are you ever troubled by evil thoughts?" and received the staggering reply, "No, I rather enjoy
them." Yet even Francis Quarles might have ap-
plauded this fitting rebuke on the unwarranted in-
vasion of one's spiritual privacy; for he was a reasonable man, as his *Enchiridion* bears witness.

It is often a question how much illustrations con-
tribute to a book. If a book be really great the pictures are of little importance. The fact that Aubrey
Beardsley made drawings to illustrate Sir Thomas
Malory's *Morte d'Arthur* several hundred years after
the book was written, while interesting, has no particular significance. When, however, one considers
the Beardsley illustrations of Wilde's *Salomé*, a pro-
foundly different question is presented. Perhaps in

this latter case the illustrator is more important than the writer, and his drawings will be admired when *Salomé* is no longer read with interest. Other cases come to mind: just how much of our love for the Alice books is due to what Lewis Carroll has written and how much to the illustrations by Sir John Tenniel? One does not realize just how much the illustrator has contributed until a new edition comes to hand and shocks all the old fogies with pictures by another artist, more is the pity! Finally we come to what Time has frankly recognized as picture books. Take, for example, the stories of sporting life by Surtees: it is for the illustrations by Leech—I had almost said for them alone—that the books are prized. Accordingly, when one deals with writings that are admittedly lacking in essential elements of greatness, the pictures may make the book after all.

It might be interesting to consider the question whether, in the matter of *Emblems,* the position of the artist and the writer are not reversed; that is, where *Emblems* is concerned, a motto and a picture are explained by a short poem. However, such a discussion would hardly aid us in determining the worth of Francis Quarles' poetry; and it must be admitted the pictures are somewhat crude, no matter how much they appeal to us on account of their quaint conception or design.

Quarles has moments when one wishes he would forget his pious intentions and break into a hearty

praise of wine and revelry. In condemning un-
seemly laughter he remarks:

"One frisks and sings, and cries, 'A flagon more
  To drench dry cares, and make the welkin roar!' "

Today there are no more emblem writers; and if
there were, no one would read what they had written. Yet there was not so long ago a class of writers
whose words were interspersed with pictures; and
these were read by a far greater number of people
than ever read the works of Francis Quarles. I refer
of course to the motion-picture caption writers in
the days of the silent films. It was their misfortune
to have their names obscured by those of practically
all the other people engaged in the production; a
brief flash on the screen and then the name was seen
no more and forgotten. Yet some of these ingenious
souls were well known as playwrights or authors of
various writings. Yet who are they, and what has
become of their efforts? No doubt their writings
will be read in the years to come only by dwellers at
far distant outposts where sound equipment has not
been installed; but the fate of Francis Quarles is not
utterly unlike theirs: his works are read only in university libraries or occasionally in the home of some
bibliophile. He gained a certain amount of fame in
his day; they were well paid for their labors. Yet
through all the smart dialogue of the talking pictures, one phrase of these forgotten hack writers will

be remembered, a sentence that has been the cause of many jokes and much ribald mirth and has actually been used to illustrate the typical product of this ghostly company. It is of course, "Came then the dawn." Now in spite of his antique poetic diction and his somewhat heavy verse, I for one must confess that I prefer to read, not once, not twice, but several times within the poem, Francis Quarles' expression of a similar thought in the words, "Sweet Phosphor, bring the day."

Henry Vaughan in a Strange Age

IN THE ENGLAND of Henry Vaughan the affairs of state and the conditions of society were so confused that it is difficult to form a clear picture of them. The contest between the Puritans and the Crown submerged many other matters that might otherwise have assumed great importance. The drama languished, fell into a decline, and actually disappeared for a time. Poets became interested in controversial subjects and, for the time being, forgot poetry. Cavalier and Parliamentarian waged a most distressing and heart-rending battle; and town and country both suffered in the civil strife. But Vaughan lived through many stirring events after Charles II regained the throne; he saw the Revolution of 1688 and the fall of James II.

It is hard to realize that Vaughan lived in the England of Milton and Samuel Pepys. He seems strangely unrelated to both, even less to the latter than to the former. Rather is he akin to George

Herbert, who preceded this hectic time, and to John Donne, who had nothing to do with it. Yet of all these figures, Vaughan is to us the vaguest. We have a tremendous fund of information about Pepys; and the lives of Milton, Herbert, and Donne are well known; but Vaughan is a dim and mysterious figure in a strange and troubled age. Even his twin brother Thomas seems to have left more biographical data behind him, though the body of his verse is inconsiderable.

How are we to judge this Royalist whose poetry was so markedly religious, and whose love poems were conventional to an extreme degree but lacked the fervor and sensuous conceits so generally associated with the Cavalier Poets? Here, if you please, is a sort of latter-day Drummond, without that poet's inheritance from Spenser and Sidney and the Italians, suddenly turned to religion and piety. He despises the lewd and lascivious verses of his contemporaries, and at the same time he deplores the feeble and uninspired doggerel written by the imitators of Herbert. What are we to think about his refusal to publish his secular poems and his resolve to leave them to their fate? Was that a form of vanity or did he not think them worthy of publication? Most of these questions will have to remain unanswered unless we can find some clue in the poems themselves. His love poems have a delicacy and refinement for which one often looks in vain in the poets of that time. His religious poems are in general greater poetry than the others; but that may have been only an accident.

Vaughan was, like Sir Thomas Browne, a physician whose interests extended far beyond the realm of medicine; and much has been made of the fact that the Welsh poet was a student of the Hermetic mysteries in which his brother Thomas was an expert. The Hermetic philosophy was attributed to Hermes Trismegistus ("thrice-great"), a mighty Egyptian magician; but actually it seems to have been a combination of Platonic and Stoic ideas with a later infusion of alchemy. Henry Vaughan translated the *Hermetical Physick* of Nollius, as well as the *Two Excellent Discourses* by Nierembergius, another author acquainted with the mysteries; and to Dr. Powel of Cantreff he wrote:

> "My ill-plac'd avarice—sure 'tis but small—
> Jove, to thy flames I do bequeath it all.
> And my false magic, which I did believe,
> And mystic lies, to Saturn I do give,"

from which one may conclude that he was a devoted alchemist before he renounced that pseudo science.[1] Many of Vaughan's ideas concerning God in nature, of divine light and heat, and notions of

[1] Helen Constance White, *The Metaphysical Poets* (New York, 1936), p. 270; and Wilson O. Clough, "Henry Vaughan and the Hermetic Philosophy," *PMLA*, XLVIII (1933), 1119. For a detailed study of the subject see Elizabeth Holmes, *Henry Vaughan and the Hermetic Philosophy* (Oxford, 1932).

pre-existence, as well as his mystical approach to life are found in the hermetical writings,[2] as when he writes:

> "O Thou immortal light and heat!
> Whose hand so shines through all this frame,
> That by the beauty of the seat,
> We plainly see Who made the same;
>   Seeing Thy seed abides in me,
>   Dwell Thou in it, and I in Thee!"

Or where he declares:

> "Happy those early days, when I
> Shin'd in my angel-infancy!
> Before I understood this place
> Appointed for my second race,
> Or taught my soul to fancy aught
> But a white, celestial thought."

It is worthy of notice that in those troublous times the mystical note in his poems is the most important. It is fitting that this element should predominate in a religious poet. Take the lines:

> "I saw Eternity the other night
> Like a great ring of pure and endless light,
>   All calm, as it was bright;
> And round beneath it, Time in hours, days, years,
>   Driven by the spheres
> Like a vast shadow moved. . . ."

Here the imagination performs its high function in enabling the poet to create mystical poetry of the

---

[2] Clough, *op. cit.,* pp. 1117-1118, and authorities there cited.

greatest sort. The literal-minded critic may scoff at the poet's, or for that matter anyone else's, "seeing eternity"; but it is entirely possible that Vaughan wrote of something that he really did see (as Blake saw the strange things he wrote of), and that in a sense far different from what the ordinary reader would suppose. What he says he saw and calls "Eternity," the careless reader might assume was something he consciously created in his own mind as a picture of eternity. Yet it is entirely likely, and indeed it seems quite probable from the language used, that what he "saw" was something that actually did appear to him in a dream and to which he gave "a local habitation and a name."

Who was "the darksome statesman" referred to in this poem? Was it Cromwell or had the author no specific person in mind? To us it makes little difference. The haunting magic of the poem remains the same. The poet's imagination still bears us aloft into regions uncharted and unknown, and we care not whether the reference is to an historical personage. The poetry here has that splendid characteristic of all the best poetry—it is inevitable! When we read the phrase, "A way where you might tread the sun," it occasions no surprise but seems rather an unfamiliar but anticipated pleasure, the work of high and articulate genius.

Vaughan, therefore, defies the effort to place him in any definite category; for the general descriptive title of religious poet will hardly do. He stands, as it were, half way between Donne and Wordsworth; and it would be difficult to find two more different poets. With Milton he has little or nothing in common. His verse is not so merry as that of the Cavalier Poets, but it soars beyond their horizon in imagery and sincerity.

The Ambitious Philosopher

In the days of Queen Elizabeth, men of letters in England naturally turned to the writing of poetry. Spenser and Sidney found inspiration in the Italian poets, learned Ben Jonson recaptured the lyric spirit of ancient Greece, and sweet Will Shakespeare made history and the lives of mortals into eternal verse. Yet among the poets of the time are found biographers, theologians, philosophers, and critics. The writers of poetry also professed prose; and here too they achieved new triumphs. When King James I came to the throne, the English Renaissance was a thing of dazzling splendor; and the translation of the Bible during his reign did more than any other one work to perpetuate this glorious era of English prose. Now to the profound philosopher, to the man with visions of new triumphs of science in a better world, prose as the most direct vehicle for communicating thought naturally appealed.

Among the writers of the time was one who was

a philosopher by inclination and a statesman by necessity, a scholar and a man of genius, Sir Francis Bacon, Baron Verulam and Viscount Saint Albans. As some men are cursed by an excessive obstinacy or thraldom to passion, so he was ruled by an intemperate reasonableness, an absolute and disastrous reliance on the powers of the intellect. Truly it would seem strange if such sweet reasonableness were to prevail in a passionate and headstrong age; and indeed the late Lytton Strachey has contended in his remarkable book, *Elizabeth and Essex,* that Bacon's misfortunes were caused by his not being a poet.

There is a certain plausibility about this theory of Strachey's that may appeal to the unwary; for there are several subjects dear to the hearts of poets that Bacon deals with in prosaic fashion. If ever a writer of prose might be excused for employing the language of poetry it would be in writing of a garden; and in dealing with flowers and shrubs, it is surely a temptation most men could not resist. Yet Bacon in his essay, *Of Gardens,* sticks to faultless prose even when fountains are his subject. Witness his perfect restraint:

> "For fountains, they are a great beauty and refreshment; but pools mar all, and make a garden unwholesome, and full of flies and frogs. Fountains I intend to be of two natures: the one, that sprinkleth or spouteth water; the

other a fair receipt of water, of some thirty or forty foot square, but without fish or slime or mud."

This passage is typical of Francis Bacon. He might almost be describing the manner in which one should write. There his style appears clear, lucid, smooth-flowing without slime or mud. However, it has a freshness and vigor that make the most commonplace subject fascinating.

Another example of his prosaic treatment of a subject which has fired the imagination of countless poets is his treatment of Beauty. His brief essay on that subject is concluded with the following observations: "Beauty is as summer-fruits, which are easy to corrupt, and cannot last: and, for the most part, it makes a dissolute Youth and an Age a little out of countenance: but yet certainly again, if it light well, it maketh virtues shine and vices blush." A far different effect is produced by Ben Jonson's lines:

> "Underneath this stone doth lie
> As much beauty as could die;
> Which in life did harbor give
> To more virtue than doth live."

After all, it takes the art of the poet to show the true relation between the good and the beautiful as well as the evanescent quality of beauty.

The theory that Bacon was an unpoetic soul, dominated by a sordid materialism and selfish ambition and possessing what Strachey called a "fatally external psychological acuteness," runs counter to many known facts of his life. It could not be said that the man was unpoetical who wrote:

> "After the creation was finished, it is set down unto us that man was placed in the garden to work therein; which work so appointed to him could be no other than work of contemplation; that is, when the end of work is but for exercise and experiment, not for necessity; for there being then no reluctation of the creature, nor sweat of the brow, man's employment must of consequence have been matter of delight in the experiment, and not matter of labor for the use. Again the first acts which man performed in Paradise consisted of two summary parts of knowledge; the view of creatures and the imposition of names. As for the knowledge which induced the fall, it was, as was touched before, not the natural knowledge of creatures, but the moral knowledge of good and evil."[1]

The farseeing benevolence of Francis Bacon made him when only sixteen years of age dislike the philosophy of Aristotle because it was "barren of the production of works for the benefit of the life of man."[2] If he was unable to suffer fools gladly, it was on account of the incalculable damage they inflicted upon an all-too-imperfect world. His ideal

[1] *Of the Advancement of Learning*, Book I.
[2] William Rawley, *Life of Sir Francis Bacon*, reprinted in Vol. I of Bacon's *Works*, edited by Spedding and Ellis (London, 1879), p. 4.

state depicted in the *New Atlantis* is filled with human wisdom, courtesy, generosity, and good cheer. It was no ridiculous nation of civilized horses such as Swift was to invent in a later age.

Although Bacon's official career ended disastrously with his trial for misfeasance in office before the House of Lords, his plans for the renewal of science enjoyed a longer life; but if one had told him that the most widely read of his writings in later centuries would be his essays, the famous Lord Chancellor might have been genuinely incredulous. An ambitious man he certainly was; but his ambition extended far beyond the confines of his life and looked to the advancement of science and the betterment of mankind. The victim of malicious enemies, Francis Bacon was, according to his friend and biographer, Rawley, "free from malice" and "no revenger of injuries."[3]

[3] *Ibid.*, pp. 14-15.

Thomas Carew and
the Poetry of His Time

ONE OF THE charges brought against Thomas Carew
by his critics is that he composed slowly and not
without difficulty. The volume of his verse is small,
it is true; but his poems never create the impression
of being labored. Sir John Suckling makes mention
of this lack of facility in composition and the de-
liberate and careful manner in which Carew wrote.
Suckling's *Session of the Poets* characterizes Carew
thus:

"Tom Carew was next, but he had a fault
  That would not stand well with a Laureat;
  His Muse was hard bound, and th' issue of's brain,
  Was seldom brought forth without trouble and
    pain.
           "And,
  All that were present there did agree,
  A laureat muse should be easie and free,
  Yet sure, 'twas not that, but 'twas thought that his
    Grace
  Considered, he was well he had a cup-bearer's
    place."

It was perhaps fortunate for Carew that he did not find writing verses an easy task; for at the court of Charles I the composition of poetry was regarded as an accomplishment well calculated to show the wit and ingenuity of the writer but not to be taken too seriously. The result was that fine poems appeared alongside of the most outrageous and worthless doggerel. Suckling himself was guilty of writing much verse that was very bad, although a few very lovely poems came from his pen. Colonel Richard Lovelace was another offender who mingled beautiful lyrics with verse of little merit. Consequently Suckling and Lovelace appear to best advantage in the anthologies, while the poems of Thomas Carew deserve to be read in their entirety.

Of course some of Carew's poems are less deserving of the reader's attention than others; and one must not forget that he was a minor poet at best. While his finest poems are probably not so numerous as the lyrics of the first rank that Robert Herrick wrote, he never sinks to the low levels that Herrick frequently touches. There is in Carew a certain minimum of excellence that reflects an active artistic conscience and discrimination rare among his contemporaries. In this he shows himself to be a willing disciple and an apt pupil of Ben Jonson, who combined a pleasing spontaneity and freshness with a classic regard for elegance and polish. Thus Carew at his worst is not a bad poet, and he often reaches

heights where he achieves with all his pains and labor a genuine poetic triumph and creates a lyric of
surpassing beauty. Take, for example, one of his
best-known stanzas:

> "He that loves a rosy cheek
>   Or a coral lip admires,
>   Or, from star-like eyes, doth seek
>   Fuel to maintain his fires;
>   As old Time makes these decay,
>   So his flames must waste away."

A versatile poet, he can also charm us with rhythmical effects adapted to a less simple metre. His poem,
The Spring, is an example, of which the last four
lines furnish an excellent illustration.

> "Amyntas now doth with his Cloris sleep
>   Under a sycamore, and all things keep
>   Time with the season—only she doth carry
>   June in her eyes, in her heart January."

Another criticism of Carew's poetry is that it is
trivial. In so far as it is chiefly concerned with love,
and love not always upon the highest plane, it must
be admitted that the subject matter hardly leads the
poet to display profound thought or expert delinea-
tion of character; yet in certain of his occasional
poems Carew shows not only a noble and worthy
admiration of his fellows but also a deep and sincere
feeling in an elegiac mood. One need consider only
*To Ben Jonson, An Elegy upon the Death of Dr.
Donne,* and the three epitaphs on the Lady Mary

Villiers. The last of these is one of Carew's best poems. The first ten lines follow:

> "This little vault, this narrow room
> Of love and beauty is the tomb;
> The dawning beam, that 'gan to clear
> Our clouded skies, lies dark'ned here,
> For ever set to us; by death
> Sent to enflame the world beneath,
> 'Twas but a bud, yet did contain
> More sweetness than shall spring again;
> A budding star, that might have grown
> Into a sun, when it had blown."

If Thomas Carew did not write in the grand manner, if he displayed no deep philosophic insight, and if he created no characters, it was because he was primarily a lyric poet and was content to make graceful verses. Rather than seek, perhaps unsuccessfully, to become a dramatic or an epic poet and be numbered among the great in the world of literature, he would confine himself to the simpler forms of poetic composition and join that delightful group of Cavalier poets who wrote for a small circle of admirers and not for publication.

A certain indelicacy in some of Carew's poems has been seriously objected to. *A Rapture* can scarcely be quoted in mixed company on account of some passages therein. When one considers the times in which Carew lived, the poetry of the court circle, and the fact that he spent much of his life as a gay, accomplished, and dissipated courtier, one finds this lack of delicacy is not so remarkable. Suckling is even more guilty in this respect; for he not only expresses lascivious ideas but makes use of the most obscene words. Carew at least clothes his thoughts in metaphorical language and avoids the coarse and nasty doggerel one occasionally encounters among the poems of Robert Herrick.

John Donne as well as Ben Jonson influenced Carew; but in general the latter's influence seems to be the more pronounced. Some of Donne's conceits are echoed in Thomas Carew's poems and occasionally there appears that argumentative verse that is so characteristic of the Dean; but Carew's arguments are rambling, disconnected, incidental. With Donne it is a compact, syllogistic reasoning or an ingenious paradox, while Carew merely advises maids to be careful if they would remain virtuous or else goes to the opposite extreme and says that since religion and a code which permits duelling are irreconcilable, one might as well abandon chastity. Of course the poet is not entirely serious but is merely voicing the mood he was in at the time of writing. Yet Donne, the scholar, has an apparent logic which Carew, the courtier, does not pretend to have. Perhaps it is just as well; for lyric poetry is the language of the heart and the emotions rather than the language of the intellect; the singing man is not the reasoning man; and arguments, generally speaking, are best set forth in prose.

Advice from a Trimmer

ALTHOUGH THE Earl of Chesterfield's Letters to his son have enjoyed a somewhat dubious fame ever since Dr. Johnson's violent and prejudiced criticism, for which we can hardly blame honest Sam, a letter to Chesterfield's mother from her father, the first Marquis of Halifax, has not received its just deserts. This lengthy epistle, which is really a charming essay on the proper conduct of a young lady of quality, was published under the title, *The Lady's New-Year's Gift; or, Advice to a Daughter.*

To the present-day reader of this letter the dissolute state of Restoration morals and the inferior position of women at that time are immediately apparent. But for all his worldly wisdom and knowledge of men and affairs, Halifax displays no touch of cynicism in this work of paternal love and devotion. Virtue is not enough; one must avoid all appearance of evil to escape the slanderous tongues of malicious busybodies.

In considering religion Halifax condemns all that is insincere or for appearance only and likewise deprecates a holier-than-thou attitude; and in aphoristic language he declares:

"Religion is a cheerful thing, so far from being always at cuffs with good-humor, that it is inseparably united to it. Nothing unpleasant belongs to it, though the spiritual cooks have done their unskilful part to give an ill relish to it. A wise epicure would be religious for the sake of pleasure; good sense is the foundation of both; and he is a bungler who aimeth at true luxury but where they are joined."

When he comes to discuss a husband, however, the fond father points out so many possible imperfections in that sex which "had the larger share of reason bestowed upon them," as he says, that one imagines his daughter Elizabeth must have been singularly intrepid to have married at all. A husband may prove unfaithful; this must be ignored. A husband "may love wine more than is convenient"; this may cover the wife's mistakes and give her more control over the household. A husband "may be choleric or ill-humored"; this calls for gentleness and flattery. He may be covetous and avaricious; and this will call for dexterity in obtaining what is needful. Finally, he may be "weak and incompetent to make use of the privileges that belong to him"; but if this be the case, the "wife very often maketh the better figure for her husband's making no great one."

Then after enumerating all these unpleasant possibilities, Halifax concludes:

> "With all this, that which you are to pray for is a wise husband, one that by knowing how to be a master, for that very reason will not let you feel the weight of it; one whose authority is so softened by his kindness that it giveth you ease without abridging your liberty; one that will return so much tenderness for your just esteem of him that you will never want power, though you will seldom care to use it."

But there are many other matters on which the young lady receives advice. Among them are: house, family, and children; behavior and conversation; friendships; censure; vanity and affectation; pride; and diversions. As might be expected, the urbane and witty statesman who wrote *The Character of a Trimmer* is not given to expressing radical views of society but proceeds on a basis of good common sense. The shallow and frivolous woman is shown to be a poor housekeeper and a bad mother, and the proper methods of domestic economy and the training of children are set forth. But kindness rather than severity is stressed in dealing with one's offspring "that love rather than fear, may be the root of their obedience."

As for friendships, "the leagues offensive and defensive seldom hold in politics, and much less in friendships." Polonius' advice to Laertes to "Grapple them to thy soul with hoops of steel" would by no means please "the great trimmer." One must be wary in making friends and cast off those who might reflect discredit on oneself. The playing of games is permissible if not done too frequently or for stakes that are too high. Dancing is not a fault if not done too often or "with solemnity, as if it was a business."

Sir George Saville, the first Marquis of Halifax, is probably better known to statecraft than to literature, especially for the part he played in bringing William and Mary to the British throne. His patriotism and honesty are attested to by Lord Preston, who wrote Halifax from Paris on the attitude of the French, "Two things they particularly object against you—your secrecy and your being incapable of being corrupted." His wisdom and moderation were of inestimable value to his country.

Without a doubt Halifax carried the doctrine of the golden mean from statecraft into domestic life and sought to trim the matrimonial barque as he would the ship of state; and yet for all his carefully balanced aphorisms and his finespun sentences he appears in this engaging essay as a kind and loving father.

Dorothy Osborne's Letters

Dɪᴅ I ʀᴇᴍᴀʀᴋ that love letters should never be published? If so, that was too dogmatic a statement, although in general the rule holds good. Keats's letters to Fanny Brawne might well have been left in manuscript, and there are other examples of amatory correspondence that seem out of place between the covers of a book. Nevertheless, we may be thankful that the letters of Dorothy Osborne to William Temple have been preserved; for they are such models of seventeenth-century propriety and exhibit so much of the writer's witty observation and devotion to her lover, that the reader is charmed by this romance and delights in its happy conclusion.

There are those who regret the fact that the other half of the correspondence is missing; but that too may be a piece of good fortune. After all, we have examples enough of Sir William Temple's writings; and while the exhibition of his love letters might gratify the insatiable curiosity of the biographers, should we be so confident as to believe that his letters also might be excepted from the rule?

Sir Peter Osborne, Dorothy's father, was a devoted Royalist and some years before her birth had been made Lieutenant-Governor of Guernsey and of Alderney and Sark. His duties kept him a good part of the time in the Channel Islands, and his heroic defense of Guernsey during the Rebellion cost him dear. When the Parliamentary forces finally prevailed, he came near losing Chicksands, his estate in Bedfordshire, and in preserving it sacrificed a considerable part of his fortune. Thus the dowry he expected to give his daughter was greatly diminished.

It was in the Isle of Wight that William Temple and Dorothy Osborne first met in the year 1648, when King Charles was a prisoner on that island. William, not yet twenty-one, was on his way to France. Dorothy was a year older, already a marriageable young lady; but it was more than six years after this that the couple were wed. In the civil conflict the young man's father, Sir John Temple, had taken the popular side; and this naturally placed obstacles in the way of the match.

The series of letters from Dorothy begins some years after this first meeting. Temple had been absent for many months when, late in 1652, Dorothy received an unexpected letter from him telling of his return to London. She was at Chicksands and not

likely to go to town for some weeks. Her reply
elicited another letter from William, and in her second she wrote: "I could wish you a thousand little
mischances, I am so angry with you. For my life
I could not imagine how I had lost you or why you
should call that a silence of six or eight weeks which
you intended so much longer." She showed a woman's curiosity about his activities during this long
time:

> "But for God sake let me ask you what you
> have done all this while you have been away,
> what you met with in Holland that could keep
> you there so long, why you went no further,
> and why I was not to know you went so far;
> you may do well to satisfy me in all these; I
> shall so persecute you with questions else when
> I see you, that you will be glad to go thither
> again to avoid me."[1]

One of the most entertaining features of the letters
is the mention of various suitors and the lady's com-
ments on marriage in general. These seem so artless
that one hesitates to believe they were intended to
make young William jealous. On the contrary, her
mild ridicule of various proposed husbands could
not help pleasing her correspondent; and if by any
chance it flattered him, the letters are more artful
than they seem. Dorothy mentions an unwelcome
suitor to whom she was engaged, but with whom
she was finally enabled to break when her brother

[1] Letter 2.

inspected the suitor's house and declared it was not fit for her.[2] Afterwards she learns that this man has fought a duel and been killed, but later reports contradict this news.

Her aunt proposes another candidate for her hand, but he thinks the dowry should be greater by £1,000.[3] Then a widower of great estate is proposed, a man with grown daughters; but Dorothy finds him exceedingly vain and conceited and does not care for the match.[4] She is surprised when William identifies this person as Sir Justinian Isham, and she later jokingly refers to him as Sir Solomon Justinian. Apparently Temple was adept at discovering who these anonymous gentlemen were, for later in the correspondence he identifies a man from Babram about whom she has written as Lavinius Bennet, the sheriff.[5] Another unsuccessful suitor is a "modest, melancholy, reserved man . . . taken up with little philosophical studies."[6] Finally, she concludes, "I find I want courage to marry where I do not like."[7]

In spite of her Royalist relatives Dorothy Osborne had met Henry Cromwell and had apparently received a proposal of marriage from him; for in April, 1653, after Oliver's *coup d'état* she writes: "Only if I had been so wise as to have taken hold of the offer was made me by H. C., I might have been in a fair way of preferment."[8] However, it seems

---

[2] Letter 3.   [3] *Ibid.*   [4] *Ibid.*
[5] Letters 24 and 26.   [6] Letter 3.   [7] Letter 4.   [8] Letter 17.

improbable that she cared particularly for Henry Cromwell, for in March she had written: "I shall not blush to tell you that you have made the whole world besides so indifferent to me, that if I cannot be yours they may dispose of me how they please, H. C. will be as acceptable as anybody else."[9]

It must not be supposed that the lovers had no meetings during the two years of the correspondence. In February, 1653, Dorothy was in London and saw William for the first time in eighteen months. Again in November of the same year we find her in town. The following January, Temple visited Chicksands, but there were still great difficulties in the way of the marriage.

Sir Peter Osborne, a widower in poor health when Dorothy wrote the first of these letters, became seriously ill in the spring of 1653; and his daughter declared that she could not think of marrying without his consent.[10] She tells of the family's great concern and writes: "Oh if you do not send me long letters then you are the cruellest person that can be. If you love me you will and if you do not I shall never love myself."[11] Although Sir Peter survived this crisis, he did not live to see his daughter married, and the final negotiations were conducted by her brother.

But to return to the letters—both writers it seems suffered from colds, and Dorothy sends William a remedy that she has tried and that at least will do

[9] Letter 13.   [10] Letter 14.   [11] Letter 18.

him no harm.[12] She asks him to send her some
seals, which Lady Diana Rich has told her "are
much in fashion."[13] He sends them and receives her
thanks.[14] Temple lends her a copy of the *Mémoires
de la Reyne Marguerite* and Dorothy writes that
Margaret of Valois "might have made a better wife
to a better husband."[15] She sends him three "tomes"
of *Cleopatra,* which she has found entertaining;
chides the groom for feeding his horse before de-
livering Temple's letter to her, and asks her correspondent to inquire about orange flower water she
has ordered.[16]

But if William Temple had won the lady early
in the campaign, he had not yet convinced her family. She writes him:

> "You are spoken of with the reverence due
> to a person that I seem to like and for as much
> as they do know of you, you do deserve a very
> good esteem, but your fortune and mine can
> never agree, and in plain terms we forfeit our
> discretions and run wilfully upon our own
> ruins, if there be such a thought. To all this
> I make no reply."[17]

She tells him that she is unwilling to bring ruin
upon him and can see no end to their misfortunes
except to yield to that which they cannot avoid.[18]
But Temple is by no means content to let matters

---

[12] Letter 3.   [13] Letter 5.   [14] Letter 7.
[15] Letter 9.   [16] Letter 15.   [17] Letter 13.
[18] Letter 46.

rest and makes a spirited reply. She beseeches him
to restrain his passion,[19] and he sets out for Chicksands.

At length negotiations are carried on with Dorothy's brother, Henry; and on October 2, 1654, she
writes William Temple that he may call and tell
of his "father's intention."[20] Here the series of letters ends; but it is not the end of the story, which
might easily have been a tragedy; for on the ninth
of November Dorothy Osborne developed smallpox.
Happily she recovered and was married on Christmas Day, 1654.

It was only after the Restoration that Sir William
Temple became a person of importance, Ambas-
sador to Holland, founder of the Triple Alliance,
and originator of the Privy Council. Though as a
statesman and diplomat he achieved nothing that
endured, though his defense of the ancient learning
was unfortunate and his achievement as a writer was
in no way comparable to that of his kinsman, Jon-
athan Swift, one cannot help admiring this high-
minded gentleman, the soul of honor in a corrupt
and vicious age. But how much of our regard is
due to Lady Temple! For it is the letters of Dorothy
Osborne, filled with love and admiration, with wit
and sympathy and understanding, that enable us to
see Temple as the accomplished traveler, the cour-
teous and faithful lover, the promising young man.

[19] Letters 49-52.   [20] Letter 77.

Resolves of a Royalist

ALTHOUGH THE DEATH of King Charles I caused many of his adherents to denounce the Roundheads and eulogize the King, no one seems to have gone further than Owen Feltham, who in writing an epitaph on that monarch "Inhumanly murthered by a Perfidious Party of His Prevalent Subjects," declared, "Here Charles the First and Christ the Second lies." Such extravagance of language was unusual with Feltham, who himself declared, "He is twice an ass that is a rhyming one";[1] and for the most part his writings are sensible and moderate. He knew the wits and poets of his time and was given to writing poetry, although his chief claim to fame is his *Resolves, Divine, Moral, and Political,* the first edition of which appeared when he was but eighteen years of age. Yet he was no mean poet, and his best known poem was good enough to be

[1] *Of Poets and Poetry.*

attributed to the famous Cavalier poet, Suckling, a matter for no small display of satisfaction; for one reads: "This ensuing Copy the late Printer hath been pleased to honour by mistaking it among those of the most ingenious and too early lost, Sir John Suckling." The poem begins,

> "When, Dearest, I but think on thee,
> Methinks all things that lovely be
>   Are present, and my soul delighted:
> For beauties that from worth arise,
> Are like the grace of Deities,
>   Still present with us, though unsighted."

In the fourth stanza one finds a watery metaphor:

> "The warring Sea can with such flood,
> Bathe some high Palace that hath stood
>   Far from the Main up in the River:
> Oh think not then but love can do
> As much, for that's an Ocean, too,
>   That flows not every day, but ever."

The *Resolves* first appeared, probably about 1620, as one hundred brief essays; in the second edition, that of 1628, a "second century" were added to them; and by 1700 eleven editions of this work had appeared. Others were to follow. In fact an American edition of selections from the *Resolves* was published in 1832.

A moralizing and sententious essayist will attract readers in any age; and if he refers, as Feltham does, to writers of classical antiquity, he will not be neglected by the scholars. So Feltham appears as an essayist in the manner of Lord Bacon without that writer's conciseness and brilliance, and also as a forerunner of Emerson without the Sage of Concord's plenitude. Emerson's remarks on compensation and circles are quite Felthamian; witness the author of *Resolves* on "That All Things Are Restrained":

> "When the Assyrians fell, the Persians rose. When the Persians fell, the Grecians rose. The loss of one man is the gain of another. It is vicissitude that maintains the world. As in infinite circles about one centre, there is the same method, though not the same measure; so in the smallest creature that is, there is the epitome of a monarchy, of a world, which hath in itself convulsions, arescations, enlargements, erections; which like props keep it upright, which way soever it leans."

Feltham feels not only the charm of the epigram but also the fascination of the paradox; and while he fails to display a Chestertonian mastery of that device, he certainly delights in it when he declares: "In apparel, especially for constant use, the positive is the best degree; good is better than the best."[2] Here speaks the careful steward to the O'Briens, earls of Thomond, a man whose love of proverbial wisdom appears ever and again in his writings.

So serious in fact are most of the *Resolves* that one

[2] *Of Apparel.*

might begin to wonder whether their author had any sense of humor, a speculation that is quickly banished when one encounters his *Brief Character of the Low Countries,* an extravagant and fanciful account of Feltham's observations there, which may have amused the English but can hardly have pleased Flemish and Dutch readers if they ever encountered the work.

The subjects that Feltham treats are those that might engage the pen of any moral essayist—memory, fame, music, dancing, poets and poetry, hope, death, history, idleness, preaching, reprehension, envy, peace, business, ill company, and libelling, to mention a few. In general his remarks are practical and prudential and not without Christian charity, his style straightforward and sententious; but when he writes *Of Preparing Against Death,* the subject moves him to eloquence, and he says:

> "When the soul, like a swallow slipped down a chimney, beats up and down in restless want and danger, death is the open casement that gives her rest and liberty from penury, fears, and snares. It is nature's play-day, that delivers man from the thraldom of the world's school to the freedom of his father's family."

Owen Feltham like other Cavalier gentlemen was an amateur in letters. He wrote to please himself rather than others, he was ready to admit his ignorance of the Hebrew tongue, and he felt under no obligation to cite authorities for any statement that he made. "I do not profess myself a scholar," he declared, "and for a gentleman I hold it a little pedantical."

Andrew Marvell in the Meadows

ANDREW MARVELL's poetry inevitably suffers when compared with that of his friend and associate in the Latin secretaryship, John Milton. One might, for example, compare Marvell's *Upon the Hill and Grove at Billborow* and *Upon Appleton House* with Milton's *L'Allegro* and *Il Penseroso,* not only because of their similar metres but also on account of the idyllic atmosphere pervading both sets of poems. One quickly realizes the inferior genius of the younger poet. "This is good," says the reader, "but it is not the best." And yet the concluding passage from the poem *Upon Appleton House* contains a description so quaint and original that it must be quoted:

> "And now the salmon-fishers moist
> Their leathern boats begin to hoist;
> And, like Antipodes in shoes,
> Have shod their heads in their canoes.
> How tortoise-like, but not so slow,
> These rational amphibii go!

Let's in; for the dark hemisphere
Does now like one of them appear."

Furthermore, Marvell's poem, *On Paradise Lost,*
is not one of his happiest efforts although it is better
known than many of his other compositions. So his
light—bright and shining as it is—is dimmed by its
proximity to that great Miltonic brilliance, one of
the chief glories of English poetry.

As for the occasional poems of Marvell, these are
too liable to tire the reader long after the event.
From this category one might well except a brief
and touching elegy, or epitaph as the author calls
it, that would honor any age. But the achievements
of Cromwell and the exploits of Blake demanded a
Shakespeare or a Marlowe. Unfortunately the greatest age of English poetry was past, and Milton had
turned from wars on earth to consider one in
heaven.

Marvell's love poems, his pastoral dialogues, and
his dialogues between the Soul and Body and the
Soul and Pleasure show the poet at his best. These
graceful lyrics, not without quaint conceits, display
originality, tenderness, and charm.

It is in the bucolic strain, however, that Marvell
appears most delightful. But his verses often present
the mower in preference to the shepherd and catch
along with the joy of summer days all the warmth
and fragrance of the hayfield. Yet all is not well

with Damon the Mower, for he is tormented by his
love for Juliana.

> "Like her fair eyes the day was fair,
>   But scorching like his amorous care;
>   Sharp, like his scythe, his sorrow was,
>   And withered, like his hopes, the grass."

Juliana is no humble Maud Muller with torn dress
and hay rake but seemingly a being unattainable.
The Mower speaks of her to the glowworms:

> "Ye glow-worms, whose officious flame
>   To wandering mowers shows the way,
>   That in the night have lost their aim,
>   And after foolish fires do stray.
>   Your courteous lights in vain you waste,
>   Since JULIANA here is come,
>   For she my mind hath so displaced,
>   That I shall never find my home."

According to the refrain to *The Mower's Song,* the
proud beauty is as devastating as the scythe:

> "For JULIANA comes, and she,
>   What I do to the grass, does to my
>   thoughts and me."

Thus Marvell takes the hayfield for a setting; and
an excellent one it is, too, with wildflowers in the
sunshine and above a blue sky. The rhythmical mo-
tion of the "whistling scythe," the standing grass
cut down—these and a host of other things call for
poetic expression. The hay itself becomes the sub-

ject of poetry in *Ametas and Thestylis Making Hay-Ropes,* where the swain declares, "Love binds love, as hay binds hay."

To return to the Mower—while he provides this food for cattle, he does not appreciate the efforts of mankind to improve the vegetable kingdom. He is a thorough reactionary in his attitude toward those who would graft new fruits upon the parent stock or improve the various fruits and flowers and vegetables. These new plants are not to his liking.

"And yet these rarities might be allowed
　　To man, that sovereign thing and proud,
Had he not dealt between the bark and tree,
　　Forbidden mixtures there to see.
No plant now knew the stock from which it came;
　　He grafts upon the wild the tame,
That the uncertain and adulterate fruit
　　Might put the palate in dispute."[1]

The fields, on the other hand, which have not suffered these impious experiments, are filled with "A wild and fragrant innocence." What the Mower would have thought of the mowing machine and the tractor, had they been introduced in his day, is not hard to imagine. He would have cared for them no more than Wordsworth did for a railway in the Lake Country. But the opinions of the Mower, it must be admitted, are not necessarily those of Marvell, and we may hope that the beauteous Juliana was more enlightened and progressive.

[1] *The Mower, Against Gardens.*

INDEX

INDEX